KIM NAGLE

THE DAMN PLAN

How To Find Freedom, Love, And Money In Your Business

INDIE BOOKS
INTERNATIONAL®

ISBN-13: 978-1-952233-51-7
Library of Congress Catalog Number: 2021903753

Creative Work by Sandy Soderholm

Editorial Assistance by
Sandy Soderholm, ByDesign Marketing, LLC
Wendy Royston, Just Write Media Services

First Printing: March 2021

Printed in the United States of America.

INDIE BOOKS INTERNATIONAL®, INC
2424 Vista Way, Ste 316
Oceanside, California 92054
877.287.7466
https://indiebooksintl.com/

Dedication

I dedicate this work to my children. Without their undying belief in me, I would have stayed rolled up in a ball in the corner more than once.

Praise for *The DAMN Plan*

"*The DAMN Plan* is the candid insight every entrepreneur needs to gain confidence to succeed in business. It's full of straight talk to clarify what drives profitability and asks the questions you need to answer to make critical decisions and take action to maximize your business success."

Jill J. Johnson, MBA, President of Johnson Consulting Services and author of *Compounding Your Confidence*

"*The DAMN Plan* is unlike any business book you have ever read. Kim Nagle uses humor, honesty, and a large dose of vulnerability, in her tailor made, step-by-step process for creating or restructuring your business for optimal success. Truly a joy to read!"

Connie Bjerk, guided imagery therapist, writer, life/spiritual coach, radio and podcast host

"*The DAMN Plan* is an excellent road map for starting, growing or improving a business. Kim Nagle is an extraordinary guide on the road to business launching, improvement or creating your American dream."

Ron P. Wacks, CEO Microbusiness Strategies International, speaker, author of networking and entrepreneurial books

"*The DAMN Plan* is a masterfully written book that breaks down the $&@! storm of being an entrepreneur, including the importance of self-reflection. Kim has a phenomenal way of connecting to her audience through real-life experiences, humor, and an unbelievable passion that lights a fire for entrepreneurs, as they master the art of *The DAMN Plan*."

Mariah Prussia, Founder / Motivational Speaker / Radio Show Host of Define the Fight, Owner of MPX Fitness, and Women's Self Defense Instructor

Table of Contents

Foreword by Renee Rongen ix

How To Read This Book xi

Introduction xvii

Chapter 1: My DAMN Story 1
   Sidebar: Find Your Kick-Ass Motivator 6
   Reflection: Your Truth—Your Dream 23

Chapter 2: D Is For Determined-Decisions 27
   Sidebar: Your Dream Is Bigger Than You 33
   Reflection: Your Truth About Deciding 35

Chapter 3: Five Steps To Making Determined-Decisions . . 39
   Step One: Know Your Personal Numbers 43
   Sidebar: You Have Money Skills 50
   Reflection: Your Money Truth 52

   Step Two: Your Value Pay 53
   Sidebar: Let's Talk About Your Willingness 63
   Reflection: Your Willingness Truth 65

   Step Three: Time Is Your Most Precious Resource 65
   Sidebar: Time Habits And Other Gremlins 77
   Reflection: Your Time Gremlins 82
   Step Four: Know Your Business Numbers 85
   Sidebar: No Excuses! You Must Know Your
   Numbers 104
   Reflection: How Do I See The Value Of My Offer? . . .106

Step Five: Breakeven = Confident Determined-
Decisions 109
   Sidebar: Visualize Your Determined-Decisions 123
   Reflection: What If You Made Changes To Your
   Business? 129

Chapter 4: A Is For Act Consistently 131
   Sidebar: Focus And Other Squirrel Problems 145
   Reflection: Is Focus Your Middle Name? 150

Chapter 5: M Is For Mind Your Business 153
   Sidebar: You Might Not Be The Best Person For
   The Job 173
   Reflection: Are You Willing To Ask For And Receive
   Help? 177

Chapter 6: N Is For No Excuses! 179
   Sidebar: If Not Now, When? 182
   Reflection: Excuses, Forgiveness And Other Show-
   Stoppers 185

Acknowledgments 189

About The Author 191

Foreword by Renee Rongen

I f you are looking to read the typical how-to-start-and-run-your-own-business book, *stop* right now! The author of *The DAMN Plan,* Kim Nagle, is far from typical and so is this innovative book. If you are an existing business owner or have been dreaming of becoming an entrepreneur and are ready for *no more excuses,* then it is time to turn the pages.

I met Kim over twenty years ago, when I was keynoting a women's business conference. Kim was in the audience and after my speech waited patiently in line behind 200 women. As I autographed her book, she was armed with a mountain of questions and seemed to have a curious thirst for information. I thought, "this woman is going to be a big deal!" Her self-awareness and transparency regarding her life's circumstances lured me in. Since then, I have served as Kim's business coach and mentor. I am inspired by the talent and influence Kim has with women business owners, propelling them to success. She *is* "A Big Deal." Kim can even make the term "cashflow" sound sexy.

As an owner of several successful businesses and a national speaker, I have seen hundreds of entrepreneurs rise and fall. I can't help but think about, if they had used Kim Nagle's *The DAMN Plan* as their instructive plan, how different some of their lives might be today. Kim's philosophy is simple, straight-forward, easy to understand and created for new—as well as experienced—business owners. Her simple, *No More Excuses* attitude is the drive and jumping-off point for your business blueprint. Packed with tools, strategies and step-by-step processes for business success, Kim infuses her signature humor and gives you a generous helping of "kick-ass motivation" for completing the plan.

Make a determined-decision to harness the philosophy of *No Excuses* and create *your DAMN Plan*!

Reneé Wall Rongen
Speaker, Author, Business Strategist
CEO, Reneé Rongen & Associates, LLC
renee@reneerongen.com

How To Read This Book

1. Don't read it.

   Consume it with eyes wide open like a kid in an ice cream shop. Devour it with a damn attitude like a tigress taking down her prey. Feel free to laugh if something tickles your funny bone. Feel free to cry if something plucks at a heart string. Most importantly, show up, pay attention, participate, and be curious.

2. Study it.

   This is and is not a textbook. This is not about creating an over-the-top 200-page business plan with pretty graphs and charts. But I am in no way saying this will be easy. You have some serious homework to do. Some of it is an inside job. Some of it is all about the numbers. All of it is business and business is personal.

3. Take action.

   The tools provided throughout this book will be your guide. The motivation, focus, and discipline will come from deep inside you. It's already there. The DAMN Plan will help unlock these key ingredients and give you the confidence to do what you said you would always do, if you are willing to do what it takes.

A few logistical details. The DAMN Plan is laced with stories, definitions, reflections, and homework that will guide as you work to plan and build a business that fits you and the people you serve. For the best results, make the time to do your research and finish your homework.

Planning is a process. It is not a one and done, at least not for successful business owners. It's all about working *on* your business—daily, weekly, monthly—throughout the life of your business. That is why DAMN is much more than a fun explicative! It's a way of doing business. It's a mindset, and you and I both know that there are just some times when you need special words, *extra words,* to express your true feelings—Wink! If I have to say so myself, it's also a very creative acronym!

D = Determined-Decisions,

A = Act Consistently,

M = Mind Your Business, and (damn it!)

N = No Excuses.

Because this is a process and not everything can be neatly lined up into a perfect table of contents, I am going to have you jump over to a sidebar, as needed, to discuss motivation, self-worth, willingness, time gremlins, and vulnerability. When reading each of these sidebars, give yourself time to digest, reflect, and *just be* as you ask yourself the reflection questions.

Watch for the No Excuses Cards! Making excuses has cost me precious time and limited my thinking. I want better for you, so pay attention.

To support you on your journey, access many of the same tools that I use with my private coaching clients to help them find freedom, love, and money in their businesses at kimnagle.com.

Welcome to my group of DAMN Planners who share wildly, give audaciously and build themselves by building others. Being an entrepreneur is a lonely journey only if you let it be. Find strength and support in being part of the community. Share quotes and content from The DAMN Plan™ on your social networks to inspire and encourage others all over the world. Please include my social Kim Nagle @thedamnplan and the book hashtag #thedamnplan.

With a full heart and overwhelming sense of curiosity, let's get this DAMN journey started!

XO /.
Kim

Wake up with determination.

Go to bed with satisfaction.

Introduction

f I followed the all-too-common way of telling a mess-to-success story, this introduction would go something like this:

> *I struggled and lost everything until, one day, I had this major epiphany. The lightbulb in my head went on and I figured out a simple, you-can-do-it-from-the-couch plan that changed my life forever.*

Then I would say something like:

> *You, too, can be wildly successful and live happily ever after, if only you buy my program.*

You have heard these stories. You have scrolled through social media and clicked on the video of the happy couple running down the beach, driving expensive cars, and living in a mansion. Just for a moment, you imagined yourself happy, running the ultimate business, being richly rewarded and living life on your terms with freedom, love, and money.

Wouldn't it be great? Absolutely. You would be crazy to not want what appears to be the perfect life. But, if you think there is a magical formula to get what you want, you might as well use a sprinkle of fairy dust, wave a wand, say the magic words, and wait for the *poof!*

The truth is, there is no such thing as instant, overnight success, and you do need to get off the couch. You are *not* silly. You are *not* lazy. You are *not* alone if you want to *have it all* today without too much effort. It is human nature to seek the fastest, easiest route. Why not? Any other way just sounds painful and takes too much time. Time is precious and, with each passing year, you feel your "perfect" life fading into the distance.

So you convince yourself that this time will be different. You take the bait and order the failproof program, only to be disappointed when the results do not materialize.

Even with a plan, you realize that there is so much more that needs to come into alignment, if you *really* want your dream business. You confess that you could be more disciplined and that you struggle to stay focused. Oh, and how the heck are you supposed to stay motivated when you are constantly a day late and a dollar short? It feels like everyone and everything is against you. It seems impossible to get anything done within the context of your jam-packed 24/7 life.

I get it. Been there, thought that. Frustrated by businesses that consumed my life, I found myself chasing opportunities like a never-ending parade of dust bunnies. In my pre-DAMN Plan days, I created a series of j-o-b-s. I traded hours for money, paid the bills—then washed, rinsed, and repeated to infinity and beyond. I was on a tedious treadmill. Family, friends, and fun were relegated to scant leftover time. I fell out of love with my business and, more often than not, it showed in my revenues, in my profits, and in whatever personal life I could salvage.

I've learned that business does not occur in a vacuum. Businesses are started and run in the midst of very real lives where relationships swirl in and out and demands for our attention are endless. You get up every morning knowing full well what must get done and then, life happens. Next thing you know, you set your dreams on the back burner to put out today's fire. It is so *damn* hard to plan for anything. It is so *damn* hard to focus, let alone stay motivated, when you are constantly being derailed. You begin to question your dream and the idea that you are enough or even capable. Alone in your thoughts, in the face of what seems to be insurmountable odds, you think, "Why bother? Why even try?"

I was being a little cheeky in the opening lines. I actually *have* struggled and lost everything—more than once. Focus was not always my middle name. Being disciplined sounded like the opposite of fun and creativity. My motivation was all too often shallow and fleeting. I longed for something better but settled for less too many times. I did not believe in my own power. I started to feel like a failure. Worse yet, I was too ashamed to ask for help. So I tucked my tail in and took multiple jobs just so I could be self-employed. Where is the logic in that? All I knew was I wanted to be the boss of me! I had an ache in my belly and unquenchable fire to succeed. It had gotten really personal.

Everything I was feeling then, I have seen in the faces of my clients. The entrepreneurial journey is not just about making money or creating a job for yourself—it's personal. I gave birth to my businesses from a deep well of passion for what I do and the people I serve. I have stayed up all night to get work done while trying to manage a home and family. I've gotten down on my knees and prayed when I was at the end of my rope. I would not give up my entrepreneurial dream without a fight. *I had not come that far to only come that far.* I was determined. Then, out of nowhere, it hit like a big pile of "I told you so."

Beyond determination, a.k.a. resolve, I needed to be willing to do whatever it would take. If I was not willing, it was time to admit that I really didn't want to go any further than I already had. Oh, hell no! I was not willing to settle. I didn't know it then, but this was the start of what I now call my damn attitude! Funny thing is, as a way of body slamming me, I was told many times that I had an attitude. Yup! I do, and now I proudly claim it.

I want to say, "Boom!" right now and do a mic drop!

But, like I said before, business is personal. My business and yours are run in the midst of very real—albeit very different—lives with families, friends, responsibilities, and personal priorities. To truly find freedom, love, and money in your business, you must—no exceptions—design a business that fits *you* and the life *you* want to live, both today and in the future. This will require building new habits. It will require perseverance. It *will* be work. You will need a DAMN Plan! You will need to work your DAMN Plan.

I know you might have been hoping for something a bit easier—a simple checklist or app to purchase. Maybe you wanted something that did not require too many changes to the way you do things now. I told you *that ain't happenin',* and now you are totally bummed.

But before you throw the book in the garbage or quit listening, let me tell you a secret that will jumpstart your dream. As I compare where I came from to where I am now—having found freedom, love, and money in my business, I can see the power in this secret. It is so simple you *can* do it from your couch! Are you ready? The secret to finding freedom, love, and money is—drum roll please—the truth.

By definition, truth is what you believe or know to be true *according to facts and reality*. It's not the worries and fears roaming around in your head. It's not guesses about your financial position or the numbers of your business. It's not hearsay, rumors, or gossip. It's just the facts, ma'am. Numbers don't lie and to move forward from here, you must face the truth, make decisions and act accordingly.

In this book you will be working on your truths, starting with clearly identifying what you want and need—by the numbers. Then you will face down the financial facts—the numbers—of your business.

The simple act of telling the truth and acting accordingly is the singular most important step that I took on my way from being broke and trapped, to living life on my terms. The truth turned my life around. It is the foundational principle of The DAMN Plan.

When I started telling the truth and quit making excuses, I increased my revenue 500 percent in eighteen months. Better yet, I have paid myself what I want and what I need every two weeks, on time, every time. It all began with the simple step of recognizing the financial facts of my business and facing the truth of my life.

The reality was that my business was not designed to fit the lifestyle that I wanted to lead. My fee structure was out of alignment with my ideal clients. I did not value myself. Consequently, I was surrounded by people who were willing to let me settle for less. Less than I was capable of doing. Less than I dreamed of achieving.

Boom! The truth is the beginning.

Doggone it! I just told you everything you need to know in the introduction. I just *can't* seem to follow the rules for writing books. But this is not just a book to me. It is a gift that I have been given to share with you: the contentment found in being true to myself. The strength I have found in really *being* the boss of *me*. The hard lessons learned from trying to be Superwoman, not being brave enough to ask for help, and crashing to the ground. The resilience of getting back up— becoming relentless in the midst of death, loss, economic chaos and having to face it all substantially alone.

Truth be told, I want to save you some pain; the pain I have experienced as a result of my very real struggle with facing the truth and making decisions accordingly. I am not talking about deciding what to eat, what shoes to wear, or what color lipstick looks best. I am talking life-changing decisions backed up with resolve and the willingness to act. This is my gift for you. *If* you continue reading, I challenge you to not let all your growing pains be in vain. You haven't come this far to only come this far.

I have come to learn that the risk of making a wrong decision is preferable to the unease and downright anxiety that comes with indecision. By far, the worst thing I have ever done is choose to not decide.

My DAMN Story

My journey to freedom, love, and money in life and business begins with a haircut and ends with the most determined-decision I have ever made in my entire life. So here goes my DAMN story. My defining moment (among many).

I needed a freakin' haircut. Not a $15 haircut—it was hightime I got a real 'do. I deserved it. So I made the appointment. Pretty mundane. That is what professional businesswomen do, right? So what?

What happened next was a bit out of the realm of my vision of a grownup professional anything! I headed to the bathroom to fix my hair. Isn't that what you do? Fix your hair before you pay to have your stylist fix your hair? Just like you clean your house before the cleaning lady gets there. (Tell me I'm not alone in this; I know I'm not!)

I don't know why, but I thought I would just quickly check my bank balance. Truth be told, I do know why. I was living hand to mouth. The truth of it was staring me in the face. Zero money for my haircut. (You know that I *did not* say "Bibbidi-bobbidi-boo!" and wave a magic wand. You *know* what I said.)

In a panic, I hit the change jar, flung couch cushions, ransacked the pockets of my jeans (even my "someday" jeans, as in maybe someday they will fit) hoping to find pennies, nickels, quarters—anything! I felt like a 6-year-old scrounging for candy money.

Even if no one could see me, I was embarrassed. What if my family, my friends, my clients! knew? What if they knew the truth? The truth that I could not afford a real haircut. Despite the fact that I worked my backside off sixty, seventy, eighty hours a week, there was absolutely zero—actually, less than zero—in the bank.

The weight was unbearable. For too many years of marriage, I had been left to figure out the money, keep things going and make ends meet. I had stretched until it was impossible to stretch anymore. My mind was spinning. My heart raced out of control. I staggered into the one refuge I knew. The place where I had gone so many times over so many years—the shower.

I said what I always told myself when things were too much, "This, too, shall pass." I turned the water hotter and hotter, trying to relieve the pain. Tears, tasting salty in my mouth, rolled without ceasing until, without warning, the legs that had carried the weight of the world for too long, finally gave way. I grabbed for something, anything, but there was nothing to hold onto.

I slid down the wall and curled up on the shower floor, rocking, sobbing, and thinking, *Is this really all there would ever be? Is this as good as it gets?*

As I lay there, I quietly whispered my truth out loud for the very first time: *My life was a mess, and I was not willing to live that way any longer.*

"NO MORE!" I screamed at the nearly unrecognizable woman staring back at me in the mirror as I stepped out of the shower. Every inch of who I was at that moment—angry, sad, so damn tired—yelled, "No more, no more, no more."

It was just a haircut, you may say.

No. You know damn well it was not just a haircut. Yes, I had been through far worse money situations. I had stared down empty refrigerators and squeezed every penny out of a dollar to feed my kids. I had pawned my wedding ring to pay bills when the alcoholic in my life drank up the money. I had faced down a quarter of a million in unpaid medical bills, watching my business die while I tried to save my child's life. I had recovered from bankruptcy. I had figured out how to get blood out of the proverbial turnip, all while running a business and, more than once, working a full-time job to boot. Now, there I was, whining about a damn haircut.

Mind-boggling. I know. Go figure. A damn haircut.

But it's the truth. A damn haircut was my defining moment. The moment that tipped the balance and broke down the door. That was it. I was *never* going back.

There was not enough makeup to correct the lines of stress and longing, so I slapped on some lipstick, gathered my change and limped my way to the salon. Having made my first real decision in too many years, I had to act. I made two commitments to myself right then and there. First was to quit hiding the truth. Second, no more wearing the "you-are-such-a-good-woman" coping crown.

In a split second, a single decision can change life's trajectory forever. Some decisions will be better than others, but in the end, we are built by actions taken—not by the time we spend on the sidelines.

Looking back, I can see the real cost of my indecision habit. I had been waffling back and forth and sitting on the sidelines of my life because I was too afraid to decide. I was afraid of wrong decisions. I was afraid of making the right decisions. Consequently, I rolled with the punches, coped with whatever life threw at me, relinquished my authority, and let circumstances and other people dictate my direction.

Oh, good gosh! I was a mess. My mode of operation, in business *and in life*, had been to ignore the truth (or cover it up) and make excuses (disguised as reasons) for not deciding one way or another. Together, these had become my default behaviors. These core ways of operating my life and business were keeping me from realizing my dream. The first step is awareness.

Full disclosure: Getting out of my rut was not an overnight, magical, instant transformation. It required having a plan and working my DAMN Plan. It took time to build confidence in my decisions. It took consistent action aligned with my priorities, none of which I did alone. I owe my success to people who, when I told them the truth, stepped in, stepped up, and held me accountable. They stood beside me through the pain and celebrated small victories like I had just been crowned queen of me.

If I had the chance to tell my younger self anything, I would tell her a whole bunch of stuff, but the most important would be, "Surround yourself with people who believe in you more than you believe in yourself. Share your truth with them. Then *let* them help."

Like I said in the beginning, unless you are willing to speak the truth—the unfiltered truth—it is difficult to get the help you need and make good decisions. If you are always BS-ing yourself and others, you get to stay exactly where you are. If that is where you want to be, that is OK, too. But if you have an ache, a dream in your heart that just will not go away, then speak that truth. Speak it out! Tell the world. Tell people who will stand beside you through the hard work and growing pains. Tell the people who will celebrate wildly as you move—even if only by baby steps—toward your big, hairy, audacious dream.

As you work through the reflections and exercises in The DAMN Plan, you will get to speak your truth, recognize the default behaviors that are holding you back, and gain confidence so you can quit making excuses. When you are done with your DAMN Plan, there will be no more sideline-sitting for you. No more indecision. No regrets.

Now that you know my DAMN story (or at least part of it) it's time for our first sidebar because, let's get real, sometimes not even the quest for freedom, love, and money are enough to keep you going.

There *will* be days when you can't get your head off the pillow.

There *will* be days when you spend the day smack-talking yourself.

There *will* be days when you are beyond distracted by life.

There *will* be days when you are mesmerized by new, shiny objects.

There *will* be days when you don't want to make that cold call for fear of rejection.

There *will* be days when your plans fail miserably, and you get discouraged.

There *will* be days when you can't believe you ever thought being your own boss was a good idea.

It is for days like these that you need someone or something to kick you in the ass, to get you going and back on track. Because the toughest person you will ever supervise is you.

SIDEBAR
Find Your Kick-Ass Motivator

"I just can't stay motivated!" Honestly, this was me once upon a time, but if I ever hear it again, I am going to upchuck! Waiting for all the stars to align and for the world to be just as you want it before you can get and stay motivated is BS.

Oh, it happens to me every morning when I am totally unmotivated to get out and walk. Even worse, on a cold Minnesota morning when I have to drag my sorry backside out at 20 degrees below zero and get to the gym.

"I just don't feel like it!" I whine, even with no one to hear me.

Hell, no. I really don't want to get out and walk and freeze my buns, but what I do want is to wear sexy jeans and run with my granddaughters. So I get dressed and get out the door. I either want to be healthy or I don't. No excuses.

Your damn attitude—the either you want it or you don't attitude—is made visible by your actions. If you say you want freedom, love, and money in your business, are your actions aligned with that dream? If not, why not? Is it distraction? Lack of true commitment? Do you lack belief in yourself? For whatever reason you find your actions out of alignment, just know that none of us are ever in perfect alignment. Sometimes, we need a gentle tap on the backside or a slap in the face to bring us back to center. It may come as a life-altering event or a simple reminder from your sister.

I can't say my sister and I have always seen eye to eye. Technically, we never have. She barely hits five feet in her heels. My little-big sister, Sharie, is short of stature, but a lioness in my eyes. Standing in her immaculate kitchen, she orchestrated the final presentation of Thanksgiving dinner for thirty-plus people. From the time she was a teen and I was her obnoxious little sister, she was always the neat and organized one. Her meticulous attention to detail pissed me off. Today, as I entered through her welcoming front door I stood, for a moment, in awe of her skills.

She strategically placed the last of the fixings on the buffet and walked toward me, reaching for a hug. My little-big sister raised herself up on her tiptoes, held me close and whispered in my ear.

"Kim, I have no regrets."

Waves of tears burned my sleep-deprived eyes. For days, we had been waiting for the test results. Tests for cancer. It felt like déjà vu. Cancer had already taken two brothers too soon. Feelings of helplessness, loss, hope, compassion . . . oh heck, I was *scared*. It was simply unfathomable to think my sister would be next.

Our father, pale-faced, slumped in his chair

across the room. His pain was palpable. When we were kids, he would always say that his legs would ache whenever one of us got hurt. He was broken, unable to make his pain—our pain, or cancer—go away for his five surviving children.

"It's just not right," he said. "Kids should not die before their parents."

I share this story with you not only because cancer is cruel, but because when my sister whispered those four little words, "I have no regrets," my soul suddenly was at peace. A split second later, those four little words built a fire in my belly that will never be extinguished.

I realized in that quiet moment that I could not say the same thing about my life. If someone had told me then that I only had six months to live or a 40 percent chance of survival, I certainly would have had regrets. My life was a monument to bad decisions, unfinished projects, things to do someday and good intentions.

Standing there in the shadow of my sister, I admit I cried for myself as much as for the impending loss. Quietly, I whispered again to my soul, "No more."

You know that this was not the first time, nor would it be the last, that I said no more. I am a hard nut to crack. You might be able to relate. Deciding is one thing. Being resolved and acting on your decisions is a whole different ball of wax.

That is why you need a kick-ass motivator. One that will keep you on track and in alignment. But you can't *find* motivation; no one can motivate you.

It will not pop out magically and rap you on the noggin. Motivation comes from an intrinsic love and drive for what you do. It *is* all you and *inside* of you.

So we need to talk about passion, the driver behind motivation. Think about this. Once upon a time, you were sitting around, maybe on your couch, thinking *I am really passionate about [cycling, cooking, gardening, sewing, running, painting, speaking, writing, or anything else you wanted to do or accomplish].* At that point, you were simply interested. You were not yet passionate.

The fire in your belly—that unquenchable flame that you needed to keep you going and learning through failures, falls, and fatigue—didn't show up until you got up and acted on your interest.

Yes, it was hard to hit the track day after day, try one more time to bake that perfect pie, keep painting when no one could figure out what you were trying to create, get back on stage after a not-so-stellar performance or even get your backside back out to the garden to pull weeds. But you did. You learned to override the pain and keep going. You acted on your interest, working through imperfections and became skilled.

That is the real kicker to being motivated. It is all about a resilient and relentless mindset. Getting back up one more time, even when it hurts. That's when the passion kicks in and you cannot even imagine not doing what you do.

It is no different when you are interested in being your own boss and running your own business. In the beginning you were or are interested in the concept. Now is when you begin to grow your passion. Then your passion will fuel your motivation. It begins with deciding what you want, then acting, learning, and doing it over and over again and again.

We all get this one life. None of us will get out alive. In your last days, the only things you will regret are the things you *didn't* do. So don't buy one more self-help book about how to stay motivated. Just make a DAMN Plan and *start working that plan!* Motivation and passion will grow out of the confidence you gain by acting on your dream—fearlessly moving forward each time you win or lose. Then, and only then, do you create momentum which is like jet fuel for your motivation.

So your first step in finding motivation is to start. Act on your interest. Start and don't give up at the first sign of pain or difficulty.

I know that sounds all too easy. It *is* easier said than done, but that does not mean we don't give it our best shot. When I was struggling just to keep my head above water, with babies in diapers and the wolves at the door, I was motivated by sheer survival. When life was easier, with no one beating down my door for an unpaid bill, it was actually harder to stay motivated. That's human nature. We are hardwired to avoid pain, seek pleasure, and survive. Don't believe me? Think about this: You exist because your ancestors avoided the pain of getting eaten by a tiger long enough to get to experience the pleasure of sex. Sorry—you are not going to be able to unsee that image, but you will thank me later, when that raw image helps you find your pain-avoiding, pleasure-seeking motivation.

I have learned that your motivator must fan the flames of passion in your belly or light a fire under your ass, as that tiger did for your ancestors. Your choice! Regardless, your motivator must have teeth—tiger teeth!

This is not merely a random metaphor. I want you to think about this. Tiger teeth are built for grabbing fast-moving prey (sometimes bigger than the hunting tiger itself), crunching through bone and sinew and grinding meat into mouthfuls soft enough to swallow. This is what your motivator needs to do, too. It must give you the strength, the willingness, and the belief to step in when your dream seems too large or way outside of your comfort zone, but you have found your passion and you can't imagine doing anything else.

Now, I've never outrun a tiger, but I have taken down the proverbial elephant! My first motivator focused simply on living with no regrets (my elephant). It reflected on avoiding the pain of not having money and finding the pleasure of being able to live life on my terms. I wrote, *I will make the money I need to live life on my terms. My terms are to live my life courageously with no regrets. RAWR!*

I threw the RAWR! in there as a joke, but in all honesty without my tiger roar, it just did not have a bite. To get me out of the rut I was in, I needed all the teeth I could get. My motivator needed to be so *strong* that giving up or letting go of my dream was unfathomable. It had to be very personal to overcome the inevitable ups and downs of life and business. Moreover, it had to keep me from taking detours in moments of self-doubt and uncertainty when I was too tired or too broken to put myself back together again.

It did not take me long to realize that my motivator needed to be about *more* than just money, *more* than just my freedom and, *more* than just my love for my work. I needed to include other people in my dream.

Since I am not a psychologist, I don't want to get too deep in the weeds of human behavior. But examining my own actions and watching so many, women especially, give up on their dreams, I believe that we will let ourselves down far sooner and much easier than we would another person. We will break a promise to ourselves when we wouldn't even consider reneging on a promise to someone else. Right?

I'm pulling the No Excuses Card right now! *It's time you kept your promises to yourself.* It's time to share your dream and let others help you. For me, I look to three groups of people as part of my kick-ass motivation team: coaches, family, and friends, including business associate friends.

I have always chosen coaches who were going to be tough on me—coaches who created an environment where I had to be courageous and tell the truth. If you have ever wondered about the value of having a coach, I can sum it up in one word: accountability. A good coach will hold your feet to the fire. They will believe in you even when *you* don't believe in yourself. But, just to be clear, not even the best coach can motivate you. Like I said, your motivation is personal and comes from within. A coach will hold you accountable to your dream and give you the tools you need to stay focused and disciplined. If you have a coach who keeps letting you off the hook, you have the wrong coach. Align yourself with people who will kick your backside with love.

For some, getting a coach is just what they need. When I decided to get serious, I doubled down by adding a tough-love coach and then I cleaned house. I stepped away from those around me who were content to let me settle for less than I was capable of achieving.

It can be tough to admit it, but there are some people whose sheer presence depletes your energy. You can give them grace but you can't let them suck your soul. You have embarked on an incredible journey. Your dream is out there in front of you. You will need all the energy you can get. The people around you and your relationships matter.

I remember teaching an eight-week business planning series years ago. A room full of women came together every Tuesday night for three hours. We weathered winter storms, navigated kids' activities (a few kids did their homework or slept in the corner while we worked) and many of us drove an hour to get there after work. These women were serious!

One night, as we finished up class and everyone was letting their cars warm up, one of the women sat like a stone in her chair, almost unable to move. Concerned, I asked if she was OK. She said she was but shared that she did not want to go home. I asked if she was safe. She said yes, but she felt so strong, so smart there with the group. When she got home, she would be told that her ideas were stupid—who did she think she was, anyway?

The women sighed a collective sigh. Sadly, she was not alone.

There are some people in your life who will try to keep you down. That is about control. And it's also about fear. Sometimes those closest to us are afraid that, when we grow and evolve, we will outgrow them. Their reactions are more often about how your growth will change *their* lives than it is about you. The most important step you can take to kicking this problem before it starts is to tell the truth with facts, numbers, and the intensity of confidence and passion you have for your work. I recommend that all my clients share their business plans with their families as if they were investors, because they are.

Remember, businesses are not started and run in a vacuum. They are operated in the midst of our very real lives, where relationships swirl in and out, demands for our attention are endless and fear of the unknown abounds. The most important people to keep informed are those closest to us. Let them be part of your kick-ass motivation team. When you allow them to learn from you, support you and be a part of your success, they're less likely to feel out of control and want to take it back. This tactic may not always work, but don't assume it won't without trying. If you need some advice, I *do* coach my clients on how to talk to family about their businesses. My coaching helped the woman in that eight-week class, and it could help you, too!

Our close friendships can be the greatest support system in the world. Take the time to develop friendships. The benefits are unmatched because true friends are the one group of people who know all about you and still like you. They're the ones who can see your bluff and aren't afraid to call it!

There is another benefit—and risk—to friendships. Motivational speaker Jim Rohn said, "We are the average of the five people we spend the most time with." In other words, you will become like the people who consume the most of your time and energy. If you're seeking to run a profitable business that you love, hang out with highly motivated people who are driven to succeed. Negativity breeds negativity, and positive can-do attitudes are contagious. Choose your friends and associates wisely.

We have covered passion, pain, pleasure, and people as motivators. Let's add one more "p"—profit. You know, money! When I wrote my first motivator, I freely admit that I was close to being in survival mode. I was so sick and tired of scraping for money to even get a damn haircut. To be free of the stress and worry that money (or lack thereof) was causing, I needed to focus on increasing my income and reducing my expenses.

For some, the idea of being motivated by money or monetizing passions, skills, or mission is just short of repulsive. Having been inundated with beliefs about greed and capitalism, many struggle to charge a fair fee for their services, or they just plain give away the store.

Whether consciously or subconsciously, you may have come to believe that money is the root of all evil, and that people who have money are greedy. They are selfish, uncaring people— certainly not like you! Or maybe you have come to believe that a desire to become rich or just to have *enough* money is never going to happen. You may believe this because people like you, where you live or where you came from, just never do get rich. Furthermore, some think it's noble to get by, scraping and working their fingers to the bone.

We all have different stories. You may or may not be able to relate to this line of thinking. You may not have given it much thought. But I do know that the conversations, attitudes, and rules about money we are exposed to from an early age affect our decisions, whether we realize it or not.

Here is what I have learned in my love-hate relationship with money. It is nearly impossible to focus on *anything* when you don't have enough money; bill collectors are calling, customers aren't paying, and you can't make payroll, let alone pay yourself.

Simply spoken by one of my mentors, Ed Rush, fighter pilot, five time #1 best-selling author:

> *When you are broke, you can only think about money.*
>
> *When you have money, you can think about your mission.*

To wrap this up, first and foremost, you will only find the confidence, motivation, and momentum you need when you act. Work the D and the A in your DAMN Plan. Make determined-decisions, then act and don't give up easily.

Now that you know the core components of motivation (passion, pain, pleasure, people, and profit) you are ready to create your own kick-ass motivator with tiger teeth. Before you jump right in, I want to let you know one more thing. Your motivator will change with you and the seasons of your life. It will have many iterations. After all, you are changing, evolving, and becoming the person you were meant to be every day. So write the motivator that fits you now. Remember my first motivator was focused solely on money and living life on my terms.

There is no right or wrong. No required format. The only requirement is that it rolls off the tip of your tongue, gives you shivers and makes you cry (just a little).

Here is my next iteration. The kick-ass motivator that has carried me through some of the toughest decisions I have ever made:

I will be courageous and master my God-given talents of speaking, writing, and ideation to build a business that generates the money I need to live life on my terms. Doing so, I will model for my children and grandchildren, current and future, a life fully lived until the day I die. I will have no regrets. RAWR!

Having a personal motivator has meant the difference between getting paid my value, and watching my business languish without fulfilling my mission.

Now, saddle up, follow the steps and grab onto your motivator. You are in for a ride! I want you to be well armed. Here's the process that I went through.

Step One: Give yourself uninterrupted alone time and don't rush to conclusions. Use the freewriting method—writing without overthinking—to make each of your lists. You can (and will) go back and rethink this, but the first step is to get some words on paper.

To force me to not overthink, I got on the phone with my older daughter and she talked me through each step and had me "just lay it down." That was important. I do have an overthinking problem.

Step Two: Identify your passion(s). Make a list of times in your life or in the work you do when you lose track of time. When you are in a state of flow, you are completely involved. Ego falls away. Every action, movement, and thought flows seamlessly from the previous one.

For instance, I find myself totally oblivious to my physical needs and completely focused when I am writing, turning business ideas into actions, or speaking. I gain more energy than I expend from these activities. It's so cool that I get to do what I love for pay! Make this list as long as you can. No limits!

Your Passions

_____

_____

_____

_____

_____

_____

_____

Step Three: List three tangible or intangible things you need or want. You might be working toward the goal of purchasing a new home. You might be working to help your children or grandchildren with their future education. You may just want to take a real vacation. Conversely, you may want to avoid the pain of not having the resources you need to live. Include feelings, experiences, and/or achievements. Think of pain avoidance and/or pleasure seeking.

For me, to be fearless with the courage of a tigress was necessary. When I wrote my first motivator, I had pretty much sold, given away, or left behind all my personal belongings, ended a thirty-plus-year relationship, sold my house and moved from a small city of 10,000 to a major metropolitan area where I was a total unknown. I was motivated and inspired by the idea of not being broke and free to live life on my terms.

Your Wants and Needs

_____

_____

_____

_____

_____

_____

_____

Step Four: List three gifts or talents you feel strongly about using during your time on this planet. If today was your last day, what would you want to be doing? If today was your last day, what would you regret not doing? Your talents often cross over with your passions but you may have gifts and talents that you are not using fully.

When I was writing my motivator, I wasn't all-in mastering my speaking craft, and I was giving my writing time short shrift. I was really pissed off at myself for letting these talents sit, only sorta kinda working at them. No more! When I began to see them as _gifts_ to be used to benefit not only myself, but others as well, it ramped up my motivation.

Your Talents and Gifts

_____

_____

_____

_____

_____

_____

_____

Step Five: List the people in your life who know your dream and believe in you. These will most likely also be the people whom you "live for," admire, or who hold you accountable. Who would you *not* let down? Imagine their faces. Imagine telling them you are giving up. Make your responses to this list visceral. I actually get sick to my stomach when I think about telling my kids and grandkids, "I quit!"

Your People

_____

_____

_____

_____

_____

_____

_____

Now, put it all together into your motivator. Review each of your lists. Remember, don't overthink or second guess, but if in this process your heart strings have been plucked or your memory jogged, add to each of the lists as necessary. Then begin to cull your list to get to your highest motivators.

- Pick up to three of your passions. Pick those that if you were to be given six months to live, you would regret not having followed.

- In your wants and needs list, choose up to three of the emotions, feelings, experiences or tangible items. Choose the ones that drive you, inspire you or that *without which* you cannot fulfill your mission.

- Choose up to three of your talents and gifts that, if you put them to full use, would help you on your way to finding freedom, love, and money in your business.

- Finally, who are your people? Choose the one or two who will hold you accountable, you won't let down, and it would make you sick to tell them you give up!

Start writing. You can use the format I used or create your own style. However you do it, in the end it must be personal to you. Your old English teacher will not be reading it, so don't get hung up on grammar or sentence structure. This is for you!

Your Motivator

Now, find a prominent location to display your motivator. I have taken a picture of mine and used it as the wallpaper on my phone. One of my daughters has hers tacked up in her bathroom. Just keep it in front of you until it becomes a part of you. Now, I see the faces of my kids and grandkids when I feel discouraged, frustrated, or unmotivated.

This is not a one-and-done thing. Please know that you will need to come back to your motivator and this process from time to time. You are doing business in the midst of your very real life. Don't beat yourself up. Learn to give yourself a loving smack or get a designated ass kicker. (We will talk more about this when we talk about building your team. For real!)

—————— REFLECTION ——————

Your Truth—Your Dream

In the beginning of this book I shared that the secret to finding freedom, love, and money is the truth. I defined the truth as what you believe or know to be true according to facts and reality. Then, in the process of writing your kick-ass motivator, I asked you to explore many truths about yourself, what you want and need, the passions, talents and gifts you have to share and who you would not let down.

It is important to keep a constant pulse on your truths. It is easy to veer off the path. We have all subconsciously agreed to a set of life rules about what is true. This set of rules may or may not be working for us and our businesses. I have said it before, and I will say it again and again: business is personal.

I need to stop here for a second and say I recognize that self-worth and feelings of inadequacy are not easy matters to face. They are deep-rooted beliefs born of agreements we have made about who we are or who we should be. I highly recommend reading or, even better, listening to the audio book *The Four Agreements* by Don Miguel Ruiz. (Peter Coyote's voice is wonderful!)

Because there are times when you cannot move forward on your own, I want you to know there is no shame in seeking help. None whatsoever! Do what you need to do to be your best self. Working on yourself emotionally and physically "as the foundation of your business" matters when your goal is to get paid your value and live life on your terms with no regrets.

Your truth is your beginning. Reflect on each of the four sets of questions to further explore your truth. It took a great deal of vulnerability to admit that I was a mess, but when I did I could choose to do something about it or stay as I was.

#1 Truth. Where am I right now? Where do I want to be? How will it feel when I get there?

_____

_____

_____

#2 Truth. What do I believe about my ability to get where I want to be, to share my gift, and live my passion?

_____

_____

#3 Truth. Who am I surrounded by? Do they lift me up or weigh me down? Have I asked for help and shared my truth? Am I ready to receive help?

_____

_____

_____

#4 Truth. Why haven't I yet done what I said I would always do?

_____

_____

_____

Don't settle.

Imagine the impossible.

Ask for the unlikely.

D Is For Determined-Decisions

To realize your business dream and succeed wildly on your terms, you need a damn attitude *and* a DAMN Plan.

As the director of a women's business center and business consultant for multiple U.S. Small Business Administration-funded business centers and community development financial institutions, I have written hundreds of business plans with clients. With those plans in hand, my clients found investors, debt financing, and even grants, but their success hinged entirely on their attitude toward the work that must be done. Those that were willing to do what it really took, succeeded. Those that were not willing to focus and act consistently struggled.

Their experiences and my own adventures navigating start-up and growth has shown me that we all need more than a standard, take-it-to-your-banker business plan. You don't need another document filled with pretty graphs, marketing data, and pie-in-the-sky financials.

Good Lord, no! Business is personal. Your business plan, your DAMN Plan, must address and make decisions within the context of the very real you and the very real life you live—the good, the bad, and the ugly. That is why DAMN starts with D for determined-decisions, not just measly decisions without teeth. Determined-decisions have tiger teeth.

So let's start with a definition of determined-decisions. Yes, I made this up. I had to. We needed both words together, hyphenated.

The word decide, is derived from the Latin decidere which literally means to cut off. When you decide you must give up other options in favor of what *you think* will be best. Deciding implies you have given a particular matter a fair amount of consideration. It also implies you may have been wavering or debating between more than one possible solution or opportunity.

Decide by definition means to make a final choice or judgement: to select a course of action.

This can be a problem on so many levels. There are too many opportunities coming our way every day. Social media ads throw them at us like confetti. Then there is comparing your decisions to how others have decided. Are you right? Or are they right?

Opportunity costs are the "costs" incurred by
not enjoying the benefit associated with the
alternative choice.

If you decide on Option A, you must give up Option B.
What if you are wrong? You may lose time, money, or even your
reputation. Well, then factor in the emotional side of having to
give up Option B for A.

Yes, this is all part of the normal decision-making process.
It's called weighing, or analyzing, opportunity costs. Simply put,
opportunity costs are the financial or emotional loss we may
experience as a result of choosing one option over the other.

If it were just about dollars and cents, it would be a slam
dunk, but here we go again: its personal. You start to second-
guess your decisions about everything. Things like getting
nichey or cleaning up product or service offerings.

> *I can't only work with that tiny niche. What about everyone
> else? They need my help, too. I might miss a sale.*

Or you try to convince yourself that you can do ninety
things at once because, well, you are just that talented.

> *I like ideas two, three, four, and five! Can't I do them all? I
> am really good at so many things.*

It's very much like the fear of missing out (FOMO). So we
keep chasing squirrels and shiny objects, saying yes to everything.
FOMO has paralyzed even the most courageous among us. It
is heartbreaking to see great ideas or even lives languish while
someone ruminates over a bunch of options, unable to choose
one and let the rest go. Or try to do them all at once. Been there,
done that. Got the T-shirt and the beer glass.

Opportunity costs are what make deciding so damn hard. If there was just one option or one way, it would be so much easier. If you have ever taken a kid to an ice cream shop with a bazillion flavors and those tiny spoons for tasting, you know the pain of opportunity costs firsthand.

It was one of those beautiful winter days in Minnesota. The sun was beating down, melting the four-foot piles of snow. I had thirty minutes before I needed to get my four granddaughters home for dinner. So we made a stop at Big River Scoop, because that is exactly what grandmas do: Load the grandkids up with sugar and send them home.

I would be the first one to admit that the array of gorgeous ice cream beneath the crystal-clear glass case was total sensory overload. For the two older girls, deciding was easy. Carrot Mango was their all-time favorite. They found it in the case, pointed it out to the server, and bam—they had their ice cream. The two younger ones required tiny spoons full of every flavor. Some more than once.

"Oh, Toasted S'mores! No, Loaded French Toast—wait! Hold on! Should we get the Fat Elvis? But, maybe This $&@! Just Got Serious!" (Yes, that is a real flavor name. It's smooth, salted caramel ice cream brimming with rich sea salt, fudge, and salted cashews. If you are using a diet app, you'll see it's off the charts.)

"Choose already!" I said in a stern, gentle grandma sort of way.

They got one Blueberry Cheesecake in a cup and one Cotton Candy Twist in a waffle cone. Whew! Done.

Oh, no! Now they are looking at their sisters' choices, thinking maybe they should have gotten the Carrot Mango. With only five minutes left to wolf down their ice cream, you know what I wanted to say?

"Eat your damn ice cream!" Grandmas in my world don't say that, so we discussed the virtues of everyone's decisions and learned about sharing.

Decision-making is riddled with opportunity costs. It always will be, but like the two older girls, to have *time* to enjoy your ice cream, the rewards of your efforts (or even to just get your business launched), you need to get down to it and decide, act, and not look back worrying about what you should've or could've. Decide already, or you run the risk of running out of time.

I will be very honest: Some of the decisions, some of the people, projects, and potential opportunities that you must cut off or decide against will not be easy. You may make a few people unhappy. It may not be pretty. Not everyone will like the new decisive you. But guess what? You will enjoy every delicious bite of your This $&@! Just Got Serious ice cream. No regrets. Just the reward.

Ok, we have covered the *decide* half of determined-decisions. It's time to add those tiger teeth. Get determined. Being determined is a state of mind: having *fixed your mind* with a *clear vision* of your direction. No ruminating about what could have been or unfounded worries about future events. You are resolved.

Becoming determined is to be firm,
decisive, and resolved.

For me, on the Day of the Haircut (and then again on the Day of No Regrets) I was determined to go from mess to success. I can feel it like it was yesterday. That moment of clarity. That moment when everything else falls away. The truth right there in front of me, not like a hammer pounding me down, but like a beacon showing me the way. At that moment, as scared as I was, with only enough courage to shout those two little words, "No more!" I was determined.

I am absolutely convinced we need both "determined" and "decision," linked together. We need the double strength—like double strength windshield washer fluid that actually does remove those greasy dead bug butts so you can see out the windshield and drive with confidence. That's probably an analogy specific to Minnesota, but I think you get it!

My definition of a determined-decision:
a decision based on the truth (facts) and
backed up with resolve and willingness to act.

With determined-decisions, you make up your mind *conclusively* and *authoritatively* which gives you a clear, unimpeded vision of your direction. By eliminating distracting opportunities, you can allocate your time, money, and talent with confidence. You can commit and focus.

Regardless of your circumstances, regardless of the decisions you are making, when you face the truth and use facts and reality as your light of clarity and the power of determination, you become relentless.

Still . . . even with your motivator in hand and all that determination, you may need a nudge. I did. So get over here—to the sidebar. We need to talk.

SIDEBAR
Your Dream Is Bigger Than You

I want to raise the stakes a bit. You are about to join a backside-kicking, dream-achieving group of DAMN Planners who are committed to bringing their gifts, talents, and skills to bear in their businesses. You need to know just how important what you have to offer truly is.

A number of years ago, my good friend and first business coach Mark LeBlanc, author of *Never be the Same*, asked me a question that forever changed the way I look at my business.

"Kim, if you don't finish your book and start sharing your gift—your lessons learned—whose life will remain unchanged?"

I sat there for a moment thinking, "Well, that is awfully high-minded and snooty thinking." Then tears came out of nowhere. So much for being a tough, hard-core businesswoman. Sitting in silence, I could see the women I'd had the honor of coaching in the past. I remembered the very real change in their demeanor and walk as they became confident and recognized their value.

I could see the women whom I could help now, whose dreams were languishing under piles of excuses and indecision. The women who were maybe not yet brave enough to ask for help.

I could see the beautiful brown eyes of my granddaughter as she looked up to me and asked, "Grandma, are you done with your book yet?"

I could not stop the tears. Damn! I have a purpose, and it's bigger than me. It is not even about me.

You do, too. It's the reality of why you and I are on this earth. We have a purpose, a divine gift. If you keep making excuses for why you can't (more likely, won't) do what is in your heart, the gift dies with you.

The stakes are that high. This is the reason that I decided that I needed to pull my No Excuses Cards, get in your face, and get a bit sassy and tough with you. If you have a dream that is burning a hole in your belly, I want you to do it. The world (even if it's a small corner of it) needs you to deliver on your divine gift.

How dare you play small? Decide right now. Do you want this dream or not? If the answer is yes, claim it. Quit making excuses. What are you waiting for?

──── REFLECTION ────

Your Truth About Deciding

1. When do I struggle to make a decision? Why is it so hard to make some decision(s) in general?

_____

_____

_____

2. Who or what holds me back from deciding?

_____

_____

_____

3. Do I take authority and responsibility for my decisions?

_____

_____

_____

4. Think of some consequences you may have faced in the past when you made a decision that was not favorable for another person. How did it make you feel? What was your response?

_____

_____

_____

5. How will your kick-ass motivator improve your decisiveness?

_____

_____

_____

6. If I fail to make determined-decisions for my business, what are the consequences? Will I have regrets?

_____

_____

_____

Be willing to be uncomfortable. Be comfortable being uncomfortable. It may get tough, but it's a small price to pay for living a dream.

—Peter McWilliams

Five Steps To Making Determined-Decisions

The DAMN Plan is not "just a plan." It is an attitude, a mindset, a way of doing business built on determined-decisions. Decisions based on the truth, your facts and numbers: your personal budget, your Value Pay, business operating expenses, and your value price/fee structure. Most importantly, determined-decisions are backed up by the business owner's resolve and willingness to act.

You gain confidence, that resolve you must have, by tracking, analyzing, and understanding the impact of your decisions and your actions taken or not taken. You become resilient and relentless when you are fully aware of your financial standing and are able to make determined-decisions for the future, not reactionary decisions to put out fires or jump on the next business fad.

You can hear confidence and resolve in the way business owners state their decisions. You may have heard or said:

I think I *should* do a better job of marketing.

I think I *could* make more money if I had different clients.

Does either statement evoke confidence or commitment? Does either one sound decisive? The answer is *no*.

The reason: there is just a whole lot of *thinking* going on without evidence that it can be done or that there is a willingness to do what it takes to get it done. There are no facts or numbers.

If I haven't hammered it home enough yet—facing down and acting on the truth of your numbers is the secret to finding freedom, love, and money in your business.

Now, let's rephrase those *should* and *could* statements by replacing *should* and *could* with *will,* evidence of how you know and an associated action.

Marketing costs were nearly 15 percent of sales last year because we did not analyze the effectiveness of our ad spend. I *will develop and implement an effective marketing strategy* focused on building personal relationships and make at least two marketing calls per day to current, past, and future clients. By focusing on high-value activities, I will bring marketing costs down to 7 percent of sales.

We are spending 80 percent of our time on clients that produce 20 percent of our revenue. We will niche down to our ideal client, set a value price that meets their expectations and improve onboarding to reduce time spent with tire kickers.

Did the statements feel more resolved? Did they have a clear vision? Do they evoke more confidence? These are determined-decisions. Decisions based on the truth and numbers, backed up with resolve and willingness to act.

Acquiring the skill of making determined-decisions and practicing it to the point of making it muscle memory (brain muscles) is nonnegotiable. The decisions you make and the actions you take, regardless of whether you are winging it or using data to make informed decisions, will truly shape your business. Depending on the path you take, you *will* see the results in your bottom line. Truth be told, the cost of winging it is high!

One more thing that I need you to remember: Your business determined-decisions are not made in a vacuum. All your decisions from here on out will be made within the context of your very real life—your time, money, priorities, relationships, and dreams. This is a must. You are the foundation of your business. Your business will live and die based on the strength of that foundation. It is critical that you are honest and surround yourself with people who will step up, lift you up, and kick your backside as necessary.

With all that in mind, your absolute first step, your first financial truth, is to prepare your personal budget. Once it is complete, you will have the dollar figure that represents what you *must* get paid based on your actual personal *needs*. If you are in the start-up phase and trying to determine whether you can afford to leave your day job, you must know how much money is required to keep the home fires burning and your boat afloat before you dive in head first.

If you are refining your existing business to get paid your value, you must know your baseline, your I-won't-even-get-out-of bed-for-less number. In the DAMN Plan, your personal budget will also be used to determine your product or service's minimum pricing structure and the volume of sales required to pay you and cover the business's bills.

In my pre-DAMN Plan days, I accepted fees and sold my soul for what *I thought* people would pay me or worse yet, what they offered. Then, like I told you in my DAMN story, I had to take day jobs to cover my personal and business expenses just to say, "I own my own business." I didn't own my business. It owned me.

Having a side job or needing income from other sources in the beginning is quite often a real scenario for start-ups, but it has its limits. You have your limits like time, energy, and what you are willing or not willing to give up. Then there is the focus issue. A Hindu parable sums up the problem of too many focuses quite precisely: The hunter who chases two rabbits catches neither one.

If you do not build your personal financial needs into your DAMN Plan and make your determined-decisions accordingly, it will be just sheer luck that allows you to quit that day job or side hustle. DAMN Planners make their own luck. They plan to pay themselves from the beginning. Bottom line? Your business must pay you, or you might as well call it what the IRS will—a hobby.

I know that may sound harsh. Nevertheless, it is the truth. So let's talk about another elephant. Actually, a small herd. Your personal money. Your money habits. Your credit and your feelings about money.

I realize that money is laden with emotions: feelings of guilt, worry, shame, blame, helplessness, or just feeling like somehow you should know better. Toss all those feelings aside.

Step into your personal budgeting process and feelings about money with the curiosity of that IRS tax examiner. You are just looking for the facts. Yup, just the facts ma'am. You are not making a commentary on who you are as a human. You can measure your financial net worth in dollars, but your human worth is immeasurable. Don't forget that. This is simply money. Money is simply a means of exchange so that you can live life on your terms. You are responsible, authorized to make decisions and accountable for those decisions.

Step One: Know Your Personal Numbers

You may have never written out your monthly budget and instead kept it in your head. Taking this time to get it out of your head and onto paper will do two things:

1. Create awareness of your real spending habits, revealing the truth.
2. Allow you to make determined-decisions to get paid your value.

If personal budgeting has been that elusive "I really should do that someday" project, "someday" is *today*!

There are two parts to your DAMN Plan Personal Budget: 1) committed expenses and 2) current decision expenses. As I have said, the budget you create using these two expense categories will inform your Value Pay. Your budget represents the absolute, rock-bottom amount of money you *need* to live, plus the money you *want* to achieve your personal goals. This will be your baseline. It's a minimum that must be met.

Committed expenses are those bills such as your mortgage, pension contributions and car payments. Bills you must pay because you have made a contractual commitment. Committed expenses also include contracts you have made to yourself like creating an emergency fund, saving for a new car or investing for your future.

Committed expenses are like your
business's fixed expenses; you have made
a commitment and must pay, regardless of
your cash on hand.

Current decision expenses are those expenses that you can decide on from day to day, like food, clothes and gas. You can choose to eat beans and weenies or steak. You can choose to drive ten miles to get whipped cream or figure out a substitute. (In case you're wondering, whip the heck out of 1/3 cup softened butter and 3/4 cup milk with an electric mixer. Poof! You have whipped cream.)

Current decision expenses are like your
business's variable expenses. They generally
vary in relation to sales or use.

To complete the committed expense portion of your budget, grab your bills and your checkbook or open your banking app. Verify the payments you are making for rent/mortgage, real estate taxes, credit cards, student loans, car payments, utilities, childcare, phone, internet, insurance, and other regular monthly payments.

Then it's time to go deep and find the leaky money. This might be those bazillion tiny little subscriptions like Netflix, Amazon Prime, the premier version of the Weather Channel and who knows how else a person can throw $8.99 per month out the window! List them all. This might be a real awakening. Just think: If you have six tiny little $8.99/month dings, that's $53.94 a month or $647.28 a year. That might be the house payment right there! Breathe. This is about awareness. Besides, this personal budget activity is Cash Flow Management 101 for your business. What you will learn here is a transferable skill.

You will notice that I have put two categories under Committed Expenses on your DAMN Plan Personal Budget that you may not expect: 1) savings and 2) personal allowance.

First, you might think that savings belongs in current decisions expenses because you can decide from day to day whether or not you save. *Wrong!* Whether you're saving for a reserve, emergencies, investments, or planned expenditures, you must commit to it or it will never happen. Furthermore, when it comes to healthy cash flow for your business, having a stash is essential. Master the savings habit on the personal side, and it will naturally flow into how you manage your business.

Talk with your financial advisor and make a plan for your future financial needs. Then make your list of planned near future expenditures—that boat, house down payment, car, educational expenses, vacations, etc. If you saved for these expenses rather than put them on a credit card or borrowed, what do you need to set aside every month? If you are serious, commit to that savings plan in your budget. Finally, save for the unknown. Life is unpredictable. Your best insurance is to be prepared. Have at least three months of living expenses in reserve so you can breathe. It's amazing how having money in savings can reduce stress. Saving is a priceless habit to form. If you struggle, enlist some help. Let's take the guilt and shame out of money. You are not alone in this struggle. Where you have been matters less than where you are going. Make your damn savings plan and stick to it. Let's rock these new skills.

"What's with a personal allowance in my committed expense budget? I'm not a kid!" you say. "It's *my* money. I started this business to make money for *me!* I can spend as I want. I don't need to have an allowance."

There are two reasons you need to give yourself a personal allowance: 1) you should be able to spend money on random stuff you want every now and then, and 2) you need to control your spending on random stuff all the time!

Here's how it works. You most likely do not have a daily $7 nonfat Frappuccino with extra whipped cream and chocolate sauce in your budget. (By the way, that is about as logical as a diet Coke with a large hot fudge sundae!) If you have just one of these puppies five days a week, that's $151.55 per month. Going exactly where? Let me really blow your mind—that's $1,818.60 per year, or possibly two house payments, a trip to a beach, or at least four car payments to replace that iffy car you've been complaining about.

In your personal and business life, there are many sources of leaky money. Your job, as the boss (the *manager*) of your business and your life is to allocate resources to meet your goals. Learn to shut off the spigot of leaky money. Allocate yourself a set amount each month that you can spend. When it's gone, it's gone. After a while, you will be like a kid in an ice cream shop, making sure you are getting what you *really* want with your allowance.

Hint: You may need to track how much you are actually spending now before you can determine a reasonable amount for your personal allowance. I started by simply documenting what I was spending for a week and multiplying that weekly amount by 4.33 weeks in a month. For me, it was a "holy buckets!" moment. I was spending $200+ bucks at gas stations for random, unneeded gobbledygook! Think about it: $46 dollars a week, and that was just one leak exposed. How many leaks does your budget have? It is pretty damn easy to lose track of $20, $40, $80 or even $100 every week, and that adds up.

To complete the current decision expense section of your DAMN Plan Personal Budget, you will need to track your expenditures just like you did to find the leaky money. In this case, you may be able to look at your debit or credit card bank statements to determine how you are making your current spending decisions. If you are a cash person or a cash-credit combo, keep an envelope of receipts for a month or track your spending in a notebook.

You can start now by estimating your expenditures, but as with everything in The DAMN Plan, you must eventually face the truth—the actual numbers—to make determined-decisions.

Let's do this. Below you will find both the committed and current decision expense worksheets. Use your financial records, bank statements, credit card statements, receipts and/or banking app to complete each worksheet. You must know how much money you are spending to know how much money you need. Take the time to do this. It's damn well worth it. Besides that, its nonnegotiable. No excuses.

Budgeting Your Committed Expenses

Committed Expenses	Amount
Rent or Mortgage	
Electric	
Heat	
Water, Sewer, and Garbage	
Telephone and cell phones	
Cable, Dish, and/or Internet	
Real Estate Taxes	
Insurance: Car	
Insurance: House	
Insurance: Health and/or HSA	
Credit Card	
Credit Card	
Credit Card	
Loan Payment	
Loan Payment	
Child Care	
Personal Allowance	
Savings: Emergency	
Savings: Future planned expenditures	
Investments: IRA, SEP, 401K	
Investments: Other	
Total Committed Expenses (1)	$

Budgeting Your Current Decision Expenses

Current Decision Expenses	Amount
Food (include eating out)	
Clothing	
Personal Care (including hair, nails, massage, etc.)	
Recreation/Entertainment	
Contributions	
Gifts (birthday, holiday, special occasion)	
Transportation: Gas	
Transportation: Car Repairs	
Medical/Dental Care	
Home Maintenance	
Home Furnishings	
Total Current Decision Expenses (2)	$

Total Household Expenses

Total Committed Expenses (1)	$
Total Current Decision Expenses (2)	$
Total Household Expenses	$

I realize that digging into financials can be scary, if not completely overwhelming. I want to assure you that you may have skills you don't even know you have. So head over to the sidebar.

Sidebar
You Have Money Skills

Take a big, deep breath. Whatever your personal financial position is today, here you are. This is not the time to beat yourself up for past mistakes. This is awareness time. When I am working with my coaching clients, I tell them that it does not matter so much where they have been, it's where they are going and their willingness to make changes that matter.

The decisions going forward will be all *yours*. Your commitment to modify your money behavior, if needed, will directly impact how you manage your business finances.

As I explore this topic with my clients, more often than not I see that they have skills they don't recognize. Here's a short story of a client that has stuck with me for nearly thirty years.

Mary did not waste time with pleasantries. She shook my hand, sat down, and started from the top. She was the mother of five elementary-aged kids. Her husband, who had been the primary breadwinner, had recently become disabled, and Mary needed to pick up the slack. She was thinking she could parlay her organizing talents into a business. Her next words have been said too many times by too many women.

"I have never worked—I am just a stay-at-home mom. I don't know much about business, and I am not very good with numbers."

Here was a woman who managed a household of seven; she kept everyone clothed, cleaned, and fed, managed the finances for the family, and spent exorbitant hours volunteering and organizing amazing fundraisers at church and school. *She* didn't know business or numbers? Holy buckets! She had skills. She just didn't translate them into work.

The moral of this story is, if you can run a household budget successfully, and on top of that, you can organize a bunch of church ladies or the PTO, you can run a business. My clients who, as they began their businesses, could only manage their personal budgets have experienced success no matter what field or endeavor they have chosen. If you can pinch pennies and know where your pennies are going, you've got this.

While you work through your personal budget, I ask that you give yourself grace, knocking down any thoughts of shame, guilt, or negativity so that you can see that you have skills. You may have the erroneous belief that everyone else has it figured out and you're the only one who struggles to make ends meet. These negative beliefs can become self-fulfilling prophecies, so drop them now before they create even worse habits!

Many of us have made money mistakes or gotten ourselves into bad financial situations. If you're alive, you have made a mistake or two.

When we stop allowing guilt over our mistakes to turn into shame, we can move forward, see our real skills—our survival skills—and make improvements from there.

My all-time favorite quote is from Maya Angelou: "Do the best you can until you know better. Then when you know better, do better."

—————— REFLECTION ——————

Your Money Truth

#1 Truth. What are my feelings about money? Where did they come from?

_____

_____

_____

#2 Truth. What are my beliefs about money? Why do I believe this?

_____

_____

_____

#3 Truth. What am I good at when it comes to money management?

_____

_____

_____

#4 Truth. What new money skills do I need to learn?

_____

_____

_____

#5 Truth. What would it mean if I learned these new skills and improved my personal financial position?

_____

_____

_____

#6 Truth. Who can help me? Do I know someone who can support me on my credit and budgeting journey?

_____

_____

_____

#7 Truth. Am I willing to tell the truth and accept help?

_____

_____

_____

Step Two: Your Value Pay

Like any relationship, if you start feeling like your business is always taking and giving nothing in return, you will grow to resent it. I don't care how big your mission is. It doesn't matter how much you love the work you do. If you are giving away your life, all your energy, and receiving nothing in return, you will lose that loving feeling.

To love what you do _and_ get paid your value is the sweet spot. Don't settle for less. You do not have to choose between love and money, but having both requires a great deal of planning and deliberate action.

Calculating your Value Pay is loaded with feelings, views about money, opportunity costs, and mostly, our belief in ourselves. First and foremost, this is not the fee you will charge your clients or the investment that you will ask them to make to receive your products or services. This is *your* Value Pay. It is the sum of what you *need* (taken from your personal budget) and the *value compensation* that represents what you want or what you feel you are worth. Oooooh! That last part may sting a bit or make you feel queasy.

Value pay is the amount of money that values you, the time and talent you bring to your business.

I don't think I am an anomaly. I remember all too well the first time someone asked me, in so many words, what I thought I was worth. Every *Who do you think you are?* look I had ever been given flashed before my eyes. I swear a bead of sweat dripped down my nose. Perhaps you have had this experience, too.

Seriously, I suddenly felt myself going from confident to comparing myself to others, to guessing what the right response *should* be. Of all the challenges I have faced, being able to clearly, and without hesitation, state my Value Pay has been one of my biggest challenges. That is why, in The DAMN Plan, *to begin with,* we don't just grab a random number out of the air. We get the facts and take the time that setting such an important number deserves.

Here is my theory (OK, opinion!) about setting your Value Pay, and I am sticking to it.

If you can establish your Value Pay based on an initial set of facts and then actually pay yourself that amount consistently, maybe even giving yourself a raise every now and then, you will believe you are worth it! It really is one of those *I won't believe it until I see it* scenarios. You can say your Value Pay is $100/hour all day long. But until the day you can pay yourself $100/hour, it's just a happy thought or a big frustration if you never cut the paycheck.

Value is the esteem that something is
held to deserve; the importance, worth, or
usefulness of something.

Value is defined as the importance or usefulness of something. Let's break that down further by asking a few questions about your usefulness and importance to your business.

By answering the questions in this next exercise, I am hoping that you will discover the feelings and beliefs you have about the value you bring. It's a bit like calculating the value of a stay-at-home-mom who's homeschooling while running a side hustle. It's not easy or perfect, but we need to recognize the value and believe it. Most important, I want you to be aware of just how valuable you really are and will be to your business.

What will be your role(s) in the business? How useful will you be in these roles? Here is a list of potential roles. Take the time to visualize all your potential or current activities in the business.

• Production, service delivery

• Human resources

- Marketing manager

- Visionary

- Sales manager

- Accounting—financial manager

- Other _____

- Other _____

If you are a solopreneur—a one-person show—you might be checking off *everything* on the list. When you get to the part in The DAMN Plan about building your team, you might change your mind and decide you are not the right person for some of these jobs. Or, when you complete your DAMN Time Plan, you may realize there is just not enough time in your day. These will be important truths to recognize.

For now, think of the skills, background experience, connections, and aptitude these roles require. Do you have each of these skill sets? How much *value* do you place on each of these roles? This is not about actual dollars and cents. This about how useful *you think* you are and how important each of these roles is to the success of your business.

What will be your level of authority and responsibility? Do all the decisions start and end with you? How important are you to the success of the business?

Think about this. Why do some CEOs make the big bucks? Yes, some make more than they are worth, but let's think about the scrappy start-up CEO/owner who has the courage to take responsibility for making tough decisions. The CEO/owner is not just working *in* the business, but also working *on* the business, looking ahead and guiding it through obstacles and pivoting when necessary. Maybe they are staying up all night and getting down on their knees to pray (or scrub toilets) when needed. What is the value of this skill set? Do you have it? What is it worth?

These next questions are about risk. If you are making an investment, the rule of thumb is that the greater the risk, the greater the reward or return on that investment. In the case of deciding to be your own boss and start a business, you are risking both time and money. You are also taking the risk of not receiving the benefits that you may have received from an alternate choice. You are paying an opportunity cost.

What is your opportunity cost in choosing to be your own boss? What have you decided not to do in order to start and grow your own business? If you were using your skills in the marketplace at a similar job, what would be your value? What do you expect as a reward for the risk that you are taking in starting or operating your business?

Take some alone, quiet time to think about each of these questions. However you choose to reflect on these questions, you must come to believe in the value you bring to your business from an intrinsic value perspective. You must believe it with your heart and with your head.

Coming to this belief may require seeking some outside perspective. Perhaps you can convene a brainstorming session with a partner, friend, or associate. Sometimes, we are just too humble to toot our own horns. Now is not the time to play small.

Knowing the value you bring to your business and that you could take that same set of skills elsewhere will give you confidence. Then the next time you are toe-to-toe with someone who asks, "What do you think you're worth?" you can tell them or just ignore them. I prefer the latter. Then they will probably say, "That's a damn fine attitude you've got there."

You can say, "Thank you very much."

Onward to get some facts. I encourage you to take the time to research where necessary before you answer the following set of questions.

What are you currently getting paid at your job if you are still employed by another business, or what was your most recent pay rate while working for someone else?
$_____/month

Using the information on any or all of the following websites, what is the average salary for the same or similar role(s) that you will fulfill in your business? (Remember to consider the responsibilities and aptitudes that you explored in the first exercise.)

US Bureau of Labor Statistics
www.bls.gov/bls/wages.htm $_____/month

Indeed www.indeed.com/salaries $_____/month

Glassdoor www.glassdoor.com/
Salaries $_____/month

If you hired someone to replace you, what would you have to pay to obtain/retain a qualified person?

$_____/month

Calculating Your Value Pay

Like pricing, figuring out your Value Pay is more of an art than a science. It has emotional attachment as well as the hard-core need to pay your bills and living expenses. The amount that fits you best, emotionally and financially, is where you start. No comparing. No worrying about whether you are right or wrong. There are only three tests right now:

1. Does it pay your committed and current decision expenses?

2. Does it make you feel valued?

3. If you did the same job for someone else that you are doing for your business, would you work for this amount of compensation?

You will get to put your decision about your Value Pay to the test when we discuss break-even analysis. Your break-even analysis will help you answer these critical questions:

1. Does your business model have the capacity to pay you at the rate you desire? If not, what adjustments need to be made?

2. Are you willing to do what it will take to generate the sales necessary to pay you what you want?

To establish your Value Pay, start with your Personal Budget. Look back at your personal budget exercise and enter your Total Household Expenses in the table below:

Total Household Expenses	$
What percentage of these household expenses must you cover with business income? Enter the percentage.	%
Multiply Total Household Expenses by your percentage. This is your minimum pay. Next, you will set your Value Pay.	$

If you share household expenses, enter the percentage of all household expenses for which you are responsible. Then multiply total household expenses by that percentage. This will give you the required income that your business must pay you to *just* cover the bills and living expenses.

You may (and should) have some savings that will pay your expenses until the business gets going full-bore but plan as if you don't need your savings. Raise the stakes. My favorite statement from a fellow entrepreneur is, "The lean fox makes the best hunter." In other words, *stay hungry*. Don't get comfy, or your savings will run out too soon.

Now, review the salaries in your fact-finding exercise. Then think of yourself as an applicant in the job market. What is the salary you would negotiate if you were applying for a job requiring your years of experience, education, and ability to deliver results? Desired $_____/month

What are you thinking when you see this number? Be honest with yourself. Do you have that loving feeling? Do you believe you can pay yourself this amount? Let these thoughts sit there for a day or so, then come back to them. Ask yourself, "Why do I think that? Is it helpful? Is it harmful?" Words are powerful. These words will infect your mind and become your guiding voice, affecting your actions for better or for worse. If you don't believe, you will act accordingly.

This is where art and emotion enter the picture. Let me show you how all this comes together by way of an example. Our business owner is Vanessa, and her household expenses total $7,000. She receives support that covers twenty percent of her needs.

Household Expenses	
Total Committed Expenses (1)	**$4,500.00**
Total Current Decision Expenses (2)	**$2,500.00**
Total Household Expenses	**$7,000.00**
Percentage of household expenses that must be paid from income from the business.	**80%**
Minimum and expected required income from the business.	**$ 5,600.00**

When she investigated salaries locally and nationally for coaches and consultants, she found that the low end of the salary range was $53,000, significantly less than her annual required salary of $67,200. The high-end in her market was $122,000. Wow! That would be great. Looking further into the experience and qualification at each level, Vanessa made an initial decision that her starting salary would be $75,000 with a planned bonus of $5,000 in the first year.

I say "initial" for two important reasons. First, can the business support this salary? Second, is Vanessa willing to do what it takes to achieve her personal income goals?

It may sound like a simplistic equation to add *a little extra* to what you must have to figure out your Value Pay. It is, but the important part is that you see your Value Pay on paper. To achieve your financial goals, you must see and believe. You must speak out your truth. An extra $650 per month is about $150 per week or about twenty dollars a day. You know how fast twenty dollars goes or how fast you let it slip through your fingers. Going through these calculations makes the numbers real.

When Vanessa budgets her business expenses, her Value Pay—paying herself—*will* be part of the equation. If that is all that happens from this exercise, it is still a huge win! Why? Because she—and you—must *plan* to pay yourselves. Far too many business owners take leftovers or eat up the reserve money that the business may need for future expenses. Establishing your Value Pay is all about first, valuing your time and talent and second, having a value compensation plan.

Using the table below, calculate your Value Pay.

Your Value Pay	
Total Current Decision Expenses (2)	
Total Household Expenses	
Percentage of household expenses that must be paid from income from the business	
Multiply Total Household Expenses by your percentage share. This is the expected *required income* from business operations.	
Beyond the amount shown above as *required income,* what is the additional Value Pay that you want to deposit every month in your bank account?	
Owner's Monthly Value Pay = *required income plus additional Value Pay*	

Just to be clear, your Value Pay is a determined-decision, not a guarantee. The business's ability to pay you is dependent on your willingness to do whatever it takes to: A, *act*, consistently; M, *mind your business*; and N, make *no excuses*. When you are done calculating your Value Pay, head over to the sidebar for a chat about willingness.

Sidebar
Let's Talk About Your Willingness

It's one thing to say you want something, set goals, and make a plan. But are you willing to work the plan, to walk through some pain? Are you willing to accept what may come with success? We all have our limits. We have unique values. We have things we are willing to give up and things we cannot imagine giving up. There is no right or wrong answer here, but your answers will guide the design of your business.

Once upon a time, I thought it would be a great idea to start a retail gift shop with two other women while working a full-time job, going to college at night, and trying to be a mom to my three preteens.

Okay, I hear you! *That's just crazy.*

It didn't sound like a bad plan at the time. I had logical reasons for why it was a great plan. Reason number 1? More money. As the primary breadwinner of my family, I was always thinking about money. More hours meant more money. Reason number 2? It's an investment. It will make money in the future. Reason number 3? It will be fun.

Right?

A full year after opening the store, I finally got a Saturday off. There was a much-needed lull before Christmas sales would be in full force. I had gone to the store early, gotten my work done, and gave myself the rest of the day off.

Finally, an uninterrupted day to focus on my kids! To add to the surprise, I stopped by the grocery store, picked up their favorite treats, and raced home.

"I'm home!" I announced at the back door like a returning hero. As I stood there, waiting for jubilant responses, my daughter whipped by me, yelling "I'm going to Angel's house!" to her big sister who was doing dishes unmoved by my grand entrance.

I cleared my throat in that way moms do and pointed emphatically at myself. "I am the mom here. Ask *me*," I demanded.

"You're not the Mom," she shot back as she broke into a dead run.

Part of me wanted to give her a wakeup call on the butt. The other part of me, woke by the honest voice of a child, went to her room and cried.

A key to decision-making is recognizing the repercussions behind each decision you make. It's rather obvious my decision-making at that time was flawed.

I was willing to do the work. I was willing to risk the financial loss. I was willing to give up my freedom, but I was *not* willing to lose time with my kids, though I did not know that until I saw it through the eyes of a precocious child.

This is where I need to pull the No Excuses Card again. *Do as I say, not as I did.* You can make better decisions. Especially decisions that get you paid your value and *honor* your values. Take some time to work through the reflection questions about willingness.

—— REFLECTION ——

Your Willingness Truth

#1 Truth. What am I willing to do to get paid my value?

_____

_____

_____

#2 Truth. What am I not willing to do to get paid my value?

_____

_____

_____

#3 Truth. What am I willing to give up to get paid my value?

_____

_____

_____

#4 Truth. What am I not willing to give up to get paid my value?

_____

_____

_____

#5 Truth. Am I willing to tell the truth, ask for and receive help to get paid my value?

_____

_____

_____

Step Three: Time Is Your Most Precious Resource

You don't give it much thought, but time is the most precious resource on the planet, right next to water. How you schedule—or don't schedule—your business time will affect your bottom line, love for your business, and personal life.

We all get the same twenty-four hours every day to use and, as Zig Ziglar said, "Lack of direction, not lack of time, is the problem."

Allocation of resources is Business Management 101, and lackluster management is one of the top reasons for business failure. Be the boss of your time! No excuses. Focus, or run the risk of running out of time and not getting to have your ice cream (reward) and time to eat it, too.

I can say this and get in your face a bit about it because I was, in my pre-DAMN Plan days, a time disaster. A friend actually gave me a name, snarky special friend that he was! He called me The Great Late One. We laughed and I made all sorts of excuses for being chronically late or not getting projects done on time.

I have too much on my plate.

Someone stopped me. They needed to talk, so I am late.

I have my calendar too tight.

Traffic.

My dog threw up.

I couldn't find my socks!

Being chronically late (a.k.a. a poor time manager) is not a joke. It hurts your reputation. It hurts your creativity and productivity. It will kill your bottom line. It hurts others.

OMG! I was even late for my daughter's wedding. *No more!*

Not managing your time, using it well, and honoring its value is by far one of the most stress-inducing habits on this green earth. I would love to be able to wave that magic wand and say, "Bibbidi-bobbidi-boo! *Poof!* We are all cured!" But it is not that easy. There is no magic, just work and commitment to creating better habits. Sorry.

Did you notice that I snuck focus in with time management? Those two are cut from the same cloth. When you get unfocused, you waste time. When you don't have a time plan (a schedule) anything goes. Especially focus; it goes right out the window.

Like so many entrepreneurs, when I started out, I rejected the nine-to-five scheduled work life, believing that it stifled my creativity. I wasted a lot of time winging it. I would be up at the crack of dawn some days and then the next day I would work through every meal and all night.

Keeping a schedule of any kind was especially difficult when my business was in my home—I was *always* at work or could always work later if I had screwed around all day and didn't get my work done. Whoa! Talk about making excuses.

The result of my unscheduled work life was sheer exhaustion. Stress-induced pain, minimal productivity, a less-than-optimal bottom line, and a pathetic excuse for a family life.

I did say that I couldn't wave a magic wand and fix the time management issue, but I do have the DAMN Time Tracker Tool. Using this simple tool for discovering my time glitches and planning for better time management gave me a focused and disciplined mindset. It brought freedom, love, and money into my business. I am not kidding. This simple change in the way I was doing business multiplied my bottom line five-fold in under two years. Now, I can say "yes" to my granddaughters 90 percent of the time. For me, that's the biggest win of all!

How you spend your time will reflect in your results, too. If you are willing to form new habits and not make excuses, I promise that you will see awesome results. Can you imagine how good it would feel to be in control? Can you imagine how good it would feel to not be stressed about too much to do and too little time?

For me, and for you, it all starts with making determined-decisions about how you spend your time. Remember, determined-decisions are decisions based on the truth and backed up with resolve and the willingness to act.

To make good decisions about how to allocate the precious resource of time, you must first face the truth of how you currently use your time. Then decide if you are willing to change some habits to use your time according to what you say are your personal and business priorities.

Taking control and managing your precious time resource is so important, I am going to give you the whole DAMN Time Tracker Tool and how-to video as a gift. You can download this bonus content at kimnagle.com/#timetracker.

Using the *Actual Time Use* tab in the tool, meticulously track your time for at least a week. Don't make any modifications to look better. Who are you trying to impress? Yours are the only eyes that will see this unless you share it. And, even if you do, chances are the person you shared with will have your best interest and your business at heart. Knowing your truth will help them help you. Just work and live your life with all its realness and track your time. Figure out your time truth.

Your needs and use of time are relative to the seasons of your life, your values, and what you want to accomplish. Throw out the idea of perfection. You are designing a business that fits your very real life. At times there may be babies to feed, aging parents to care for, full-time jobs to do, employee no-shows to cover, bills to pay, and laundry to address. There will be hungry gremlins ready to eat up your time. There will be time you gladly give away and time you must hoard for sanity's sake. To those gremlins who try to steal your time, just say NO.

No is the best two-letter word in the English language. If used properly, it honors your priorities and puts the most important people and activities first. Having a plan makes saying no to time wasters and time takers much easier. It all comes down to *you* making a determined-decision about how you spend your time and then consistently working your self-set schedule to the best of your ability. Give yourself grace but take care not to make excuses.

No matter whether you discover you have been wasting an exorbitant number of hours or not, the most important thing is awareness. When I first tracked time, I calculated that I wasted at least 500 hours per year driving needlessly. I multiplied 500 by my billable hourly rate. Gulp! I could've been sitting on a beach somewhere with change to spare and a good haircut.

Here's the kicker: When you start time tracking, you have to give yourself time to do it. [Insert your favorite eye roll emoji.] I know what you're thinking. You are trying to find time to get your work done—there is no time to track time. What can I say? Just make it and take it. It will be damn well worth the effort. From here forward, I am going to make the bold assumption that you have done or will do your time tracking. After all, here you are trying to find freedom, love, and money in your business, and this is a nonnegotiable step. So, go download the DAMN Time Tracker Tool and know your time truth, right now.

Now that you have the truth about how you spend your time, how does it make you feel? Are you happy? Are you disappointed? Are you surprised? Do you feel like it really wouldn't matter if you developed new habits or not? Do you feel like it's out of your control? Do you think this life is just too crazy and unpredictable?

I am not going to tell you to buck up or get over it. Getting a handle on time use is one of the hardest habits you will ever form. All I know is if you accept chaos as the norm, chaos you get. In the DAMN Time Tracker Tool, you have the opportunity to write out your reflections and answers to the questions that I posed in the previous paragraph. You know the drill: make and take the time for this reflection.

Writing out my time plan helped me make sure that I was not only scheduling myself to work during my most productive hours, but also ensure I was not trying to squeeze my personal life and family (my top two priorities) into leftover time. Telling the truth about my available time was a critical step to designing my business model. I had to recognize that unless I was, in fact, Superwoman and could spin the planet backward to get more time, there were only twenty-four hours in a day.

The DAMN Time Tracker Tool will also have you dig deeper into time use habits that you may want to modify. You will also explore your willingness to do what it will take to make the changes. Work through the Time Use, Habits and Productivity step in the tool then move on to decide what you can outsource or delegate.

What could be outsourced or delegated?			
Time Consuming Task or Activity	Yes	No	To Whom?
Bookkeeping	X		Virtual assistant
Social Media	X		Marketing Manager
Dishes	X		family
Laundry	X		family

Delegating and outsourcing can be tough. Especially if you are a control freak and perfectionist. Regardless, it is quite possible that someone else could take over some of your work and just maybe do it better than you! As you review everything that you take on in a week, ask yourself these two simple questions. Are you the best person for the job? Was it a good use of your time (really)?

Time Use, Habits, and Productivity			
		Check one	
Time Use	Time Spent*	I am willing to create a new habit	I am unwilling to create a new habit
Social Media	12.00		
TV, YouTube, or livestream	10.00		
Driving	15.00		
Waiting	3.00		
Giving away time—not saying no	6.00		
Finding lost items or files	2.00		
Unproductive chats during productivity time	8.00		
Total Time Used	56.00		

For example: If you outsourced your web design or bookkeeping and use the hours as billable client hours or to get some sleep, would it be worth it? Or at a minimum, if you delegated folding the towels to your kids, what would be wrong with the towels getting put in the linen closet regardless of how they got folded? Let go of perfection in some areas and seek out the best help you can get in others. It is worth the effort and investment. First, you must be willing to ask for and receive help. Second, you must recognize that done is better than perfect.

Before you dig in and develop your own DAMN Time Plan, the tool will ask you one more question. This is a biggie! Are you using your time according to your priorities? This can be a slap upside the head. You say you want this business. You want freedom, love, and money. You want a life but just maybe your time use does not reflect this desire. It's a wake-up call. You either want this dream or you don't. You can make excuses until you are blue in the face or make some changes.

I know this is hardcore. It was for me, too. The DAMN Time Tracker exercise is all about discovery. The decisions are all yours going forward. Remember, you are responsible, and it does not matter how you have behaved in the past. Its how you will behave today and into the future that matters.

Ask yourself these questions as you reflect on how you did or didn't prioritize your time. Did you have a plan but then gave away the time? Did you run out of time because you procrastinated by following unproductive bunny trails and doing projects that weren't on the plan? Are you just trying to work during the wrong hours? Have you planned for the unexpected? Are you simply trying to do too much in the 24-7 you have?

In thirty years of business, I have screwed up and taken on more than I could do, put my family second, and followed more than my fair share of those bunny trails. Now that I know better, I do better. I designed my business to fit my life and my priorities. For example, when I cared for my mom, I had to adjust my life completely. Part of my DAMN Plan for freedom, love, and money is to be able to really put my family first. My business and my DAMN Time Plan are designed accordingly. The time I got to spend with my mom, hearing her stories and seeing the world through her beautiful eyes of age was priceless. Work and business will always be there. Lost time can never be retrieved.

There may be days when time is twisted and you just simply can't make it all work. For days like this, make an agreement with yourself to always do your best. Your best will vary from day-to-day, so give yourself grace, but quit making excuses for time use within your control.

Scheduling time to honor your priorities is an important step. Take a hard look at how you use your time. Answer yes or no. Is your time use in alignment with your priorities?

If the answer is no, remember perfection does not exist and that where you are going is more important than where you have been. Be patient with yourself. Getting your damn time on track will take a number of iterations before you get it right.

Now you are ready to develop your DAMN Time Plan. Using the following questions, start making some determined-decisions about how you will spend your time resources. You may have additional questions that are unique to your time use. Give yourself ample time for this exercise.

- When do you work most productively, staying focused and disciplined for creative development work?

- When is the best time to devote to direct client work? When do your clients need you? What are the best hours to be open?

- How many billable hours must you have to meet your current revenue or production goals? Block out the time. If you don't devote this time, how are you going to pay the bills?

- When and how will you get your financials done? Will you use a bookkeeper/accountant?

- How or when will you get your marketing done? Can client contacts, emails, social media, mailers, networking, etc., be outsourced?

- What do your family or loved ones need? If family is a priority for you, schedule them. No leaving priorities to leftover time.

- What are your health, spiritual, and wellness goals? When are the optimal times to work out, to walk, to meditate, or to just be? Self-care is important. I consider it nonnegotiable for the health of my business. An exhausted, mentally drained business owner is an unproductive business owner.

Using the *My DAMN Time Plan* tab in tool, start by scheduling in your very real life first. Claiming a personal life really is the beauty of being your own boss—if you plan your business around it! Schedule time for sleep, meals, mental and physical health care, family, faith, and social/community time. The way to stay in love with your business is to be in love with your life. If you feel like one is being strangled by the other, you will grow to hate both. Be proactive. Tell the truth about what you need. Don't accept the notion that you must squeeze your life and loves into leftover time.

Here are four nonnegotiable activities that must be in your time plan.

1. You have to sleep; six to eight hours is the healthiest.

2. You have to break to eat; eating on the fly is unhealthy.

3. You have to schedule physical activity; twenty minutes per day minimum.

4. You must have time for you and your loves.

Now, make a schedule for your business. I know, I know, you are still trying to reject the traditional work life, but there are no ifs, ands, or buts about it: having a schedule works by reducing the stress that comes with chaotic time habits. Just try it!

Your schedule does not have to be nine to five, with a lunch break at noon and coffee at ten. This is *your* schedule, and its only requirement is enough hours available and designated to complete the work of the business. Maybe you work around a kid's schedule, your internal clock, or when clients are available. Just remember that this is your business. You are the boss. You make the schedule. You're authorized and responsible.

Though I could work anytime and anywhere, at a minimum, I start work at 8 a.m. every day. I work five days a week and weekends as required for speaking or training engagements. I do not do all-nighters, and I restrict myself to working no later than 10 p.m. This schedule is based on my life priorities and my most effective work hours.

Like all habits, to make them work, you must act in a consistent manner until your body and mind just simply are on autopilot and you naturally rock and roll when the time comes. I mentioned before that stress-induced pain is often a result of poor time management. Our bodies *do* like it when things are predictable at least part of the time. Your body will love you for keeping a schedule, and it will reward you by not distracting you with physical ailments.

Leave some unscheduled time. I call this gray space. Like any plan, when it is so restrictive that you can't move, you reject it. It's like when the doctor tells me, "no more chocolate." You know exactly what I will crave. Leave plenty of time for the unknown, the unplanned, or just nothing—just *being*. If you are packing your days wall to wall, go back and say no to something. You only have twenty-four hours in each day and one life to live.

The biggest obstacle to sticking to your schedule will be you! You will be the hardest person you have ever supervised. You may need to find someone to hold you accountable. Go back to your kickass motivator. Did you choose someone who will be "your person"? If not, the best way to form a new habit is to tell someone who will not let you off the hook if you slack.

You can see a sample of one of my DAMN Time Plans in the DAMN Time Tracker Tool. It's the plan that got me back on track. For me to get real with my business, I had to *take time* and do what I decided was important. I had to quit squeezing priorities into leftover time. If I couldn't do that, I had to admit my dreams and what I wanted to accomplish were not important. That was a tough pill to swallow.

We need to talk about time gremlins. Those cute little monsters that you must not feed. Head over to the sidebar. Let's talk about them.

Sidebar

Time Habits And Other Gremlins

To avoid being honest with ourselves, we use events, people, places, and things as reasons (excuses in disguise) for why we didn't do what we said we would do. No doubt, there are real bumps and jiggles along the way—the unexpected is inevitable. There will be what seems like insurmountable challenges. It will be up to you to grab onto your motivator and replace your current habits with self-imposed discipline.

This is a good time to remind you that if you haven't done your DAMN Time Plan yet, *now is the time!* You can't tame your time gremlins without first recognizing them for what they are: darling monsters.

Time gremlins raid our lives, enticing us to get off track. You know, like Facebook, YouTube, LinkedIn, Instagram, Pinterest, email, etc. Like your dirty laundry and the dishes in the sink, they will *all* still be there when you are done doing what you said you would do.

Heaven forbid I should tell you not to go on Facebook, LinkedIn, or Instagram! I want to connect with you there, but get a grip. Social media itself is not the gremlin, it's how you are using it. It's your habits. If your use is out of hand, get control of it. (Your smart phone can even tell you when enough is enough!)

OK, I admit to a small addiction to Netflix. Netflix is a time gremlin for me. Sorry, Leroy Jethro Gibbs and *NCIS* reruns—you've gotta go! The moment I realized that I had wasted six hours a day for a week, forty-two hours that I could never get back, watching Jethro, I had to get serious about my time use. As cute as Mark Harmon is, watching him solve one murder right after another was not a good use of my time. Besides, if I can write five hundred words an hour, I could have, theoretically, popped-out a twenty-thousand-word book in that lost forty-two hours. I cancelled my subscription and gave my TV away. I have better things to do.

There are demands on our time that feel like they are outside our control. My biggie was saying *yes* when I should have said *no*. Caught up in a vicious, codependent cycle of putting high value on helping others, I never said *no*. This cost me precious time, and I let people down when I couldn't fulfill my promises or did a half-assed job for lack of time.

I know I am not alone in this; we worry about offending or hurting the asker. We worry something bad will happen if we don't jump in and save them or the day. Then our egos rear their ugly heads, making us think if we don't do the project, it won't get done right. (This is codependency at its best.)

I want to say yes as often as I can. I also want to say no when it's the best response. Here is my take on the power of saying no: When you say no, you empower the person who is requesting your time by making them responsible for solving their own problems. When you say no to requests that do not align with your direction, you solidify the importance of your mission in your mind. Most importantly, when you value your time, you value yourself, and that trickles down, empowering others to do the same.

Learning to say no is a skill to be learned. Quick tip: When you are about to say yes when you shouldn't, instead say, "Thank you for asking. I am unable to help (or I know a better person for the job)." There is no need for excuses or debate. Just say no.

Sounds easy, right? Oh, heck no! There are people who excel in the art of guilting. For these people and situations, you will need help. You will need a DAMN Plan, your DAMN Time Plan. I use my plan and a team of ass-kickers to back me up when I can't say no on my own.

Earlier, we talked about assembling a team. Who will be your ass-kicker? Is this person on the team already? Have you given him or her permission to help you beat your time gremlins? In the acknowledgments of this book, I shared mine. I can say without hesitation there is no way I would have finished this book without her. I was lucky enough to give birth to mine. Go find *your* own Sandy.

One more time gremlin that bites solopreneurs and home-based businesses in the backside is their workspace. You may have walked away from a structured office environment to start your business, but now more than ever, the space where you work needs to be structured and organized. You cannot afford to be disorganized.

Let's imagine a scenario. You have settled at your desk, are ready to work and, damn, where did that file go? Then you spend thirty minutes shuffling stuff around, searching Dropbox, and then you start rifling through the two-week stack of junk mail. Double damn! Where did it go? Oh, yeah, they sent it to me via email. Now you are searching through the 4,999 random emails currently in your inbox. Another thirty minutes go by as you get distracted by a couple emails you haven't read yet.

Let's say this occurs three times per week. That's three lost hours per week, times fifty weeks. That's 150 hours! Now multiply that by your billable rate! Let that sink in for a moment. Damn!

This everyday occurrence doesn't include distractions like dirty dishes, laundry, pets, and kids, not to mention calls from friends and family who think you can drop everything because you work from home or don't have a "real" job.

I love working from home. I loved it when I was working between diaper changes, meal prep, and laundry. I love it now with only myself as a distraction. To preserve the love of your business and your sanity, here are my three best tips if you are home-officed.

1. Create a space to work that you can go to and walk away from, preferably in a room with a door. Start and end your workday at the same time as often as you can. I know this flies in the

face of that freedom you want, but it will save you precious time. After all, this is the reason you left your nine-to-five job. You want more time for life.

2. Wherever you work, even if your desk is just the desktop of your laptop, set aside ten minutes at the end of the day to organize your desk (desktop or online files) and prepare for the next day.

   Most people won't do this because they can't see an immediate payoff. At first, it's just a pain, kind of like exercise is for the first couple weeks. But it won't take as long to experience the benefit of coming back to a space you don't have to clean before you can work. Don't forget about the amount of time and money you lost in our above scenario just searching for a file.

3. Learn to say, "I'm working!" Learn to say it with authority and without apology. Would you apologize if you were working for an employer other than yourself?

──────── REFLECTION ────────

Your Time Gremlins

We've talked about a few of my time gremlins, but you will have your own unique list. To conquer them, I suggest you simply make a list of your little time thieves.

Time Gremlin	Control/No Control	Delegate, Share, Kick To The Curb	Who Can Help?

Now go back and mark the time gremlins on your list that are within your control and those outside of your control. Mark which of the gremlins you can delegate, share, or kick to the curb. Write the name of the person(s) who could help next to those gremlins you could delegate or share.

Last, reflect on any thoughts that may be floating around in your head.

1. Why might this delegation and sharing not work? How can I make it work?

2. What will it feel like when I get my time gremlins under control?

3. How will those around me react?

4. How will I keep my time gremlins from rearing their furry little heads? (Maybe it's your kick-ass motivator. It just might need bigger teeth to fight off your gremlins.).

Sometimes, change requires drastic measures. I gave away a brand-new 43-inch smart TV and threw my *NCIS* gremlin out the window. Even that didn't work some days. Because, I simply traded one distraction for another. My ass-kicker, who is my business partner AND daughter put a stop to that when she said, "No going out with your boyfriend until you get your work done!" Yikes! That was a turning of the tables. I think I said that to her once or twice in her teen years. I had a good laugh and put the pedal to the metal.

Who can you enlist for help that will be as relentless as *my Sandy* when you get off track and unfocused? Choose wisely.

Find something you love to do and you'll never have to work a day in your life.

Step Four: Know Your Business Numbers

Guess how I decided what my fee structure should look like in my very first *real* business! Come on, guess!

OK, I'll let you in on my secret: I borrowed my sister's price list. I know, I know. Just saying it sounds so wrong in so many ways. For real, though, that's what I did. I landed a contract with J. C. Penney with it.

I was working as an interior decorator at a JCP Custom Decorating Studio. I was twenty-four years old, and thought I knew a whole lot more than the general manager, with thirty years of experience. Yup! I had a damn attitude back then, too.

Tired of his tirades about losing money, I figured out how to solve a major manufacturing and shipping problem. I would start a local fabrication workroom. I could save them money—a lot of money—if they didn't have to ship their one-of-a-kind draperies and decorating items across the entire country by semitruck. They could save even more money if the inevitable corrections to custom products could be made on-site. I knew how to make draperies and pretty much anything that could be sewn, so like an entrepreneur-in-heat and without any plan at all, I marched into the general manager's office and said, "I have a solution for your problem!"

I am not sure if he was desperate or intrigued, but he immediately asked for my price list. Then he asked, "How do you charge for a lambrequin? By the square foot or linear foot?"

What the heck is a *lambrequin*? Until that moment, I had never even heard the word. If you want to know what it is, Google it.

I smiled and looked the man right in the eyes and said, "Let me get back to you on pricing. Knowing what I know about this studio's needs, I want to be sure my fee structure works for both of us. I can fax (obviously, this was a while ago!) you a copy of my price list tomorrow."

If I had nothing else going for me, at least I had the lingo down.

I called my other big sister, a newly minted entrepreneur herself, with a drapery workroom close to Dallas, Texas. "Vicky, I just did this *thing*. I think I might be able to get a contract with J. C. Penney. Can I get a copy of your price list?"

I changed the headings and faxed "my" price list to the general manager. He didn't even blink. He just nodded, smiled like the Cheshire Cat and said, "Sounds good. I will have a contract for you to sign in a week."

Damn!

I still didn't have a plan other than the thoughts I was holding between my ears. I didn't know if the prices were right or wrong. I was using Dallas pricing in Bismarck, North Dakota. I didn't know about the cost of goods sold, a.k.a. variable expenses. I had no idea what my fixed expenses would be. Oh, and did I tell you that I only had an extra $50 to spend on this proposition? So I bought a ping-pong table.

Now I have your head spinning. Yes, I was making it all up as I went. Regardless, from what I have seen in thirty years of coaching, I was totally normal.

Back to the ping-pong table. It was foldable and I modified it to use as a cutting table. If Pinterest had been around then, I would have been a sensation. I set it up smack-dab in the middle of my living room. It also served as a pretty good playhouse for my daughter. Bonus!

I had the pedal to the floorboards establishing my previously nonexistent workroom. I received fabrics and work orders one week after I spouted those infamous words, "I have a solution for your problem."

I did not know what I didn't know. That might have been my saving grace. In my first year, if I am 100 percent honest, I just got lucky. I only had two things going for me: 1) the lingo, and 2) I am a damn good seamstress. Other than that, I did not know if I was really making money on any one given day, until Tax Day.

I was not alone or abnormal in not knowing my numbers. According to a 2019 Bank of America study, 84 percent of small business owners do not have a financial plan, do not understand the implications of cash flow, and pretty much just grab their prices out of the air. There is a lot of winging it going on out there!

They might have everything set up in QuickBooks or some other accounting system, but they never analyze their numbers to see if they are on the right path and making the right decisions. They have no way of making real, determined-decisions because they *think*; they don't *know*. They don't know their numbers.

Unlike twenty-four-year-old me and other entrepreneurs-in-heat, you *do* need to have a plan. Attitude is good, but if you have an attitude with a plan—wowza! Get out of the way, DAMN Planner coming through!

In Step Four, we will cover the critical numbers you need to know. This is another nonnegotiable, so no excuses.

1. Variable Costs

2. Fixed costs

3. Pricing

When you get all of these numbers together for your business, you will analyze your personal numbers, including your Value Pay and your business numbers using a break-even formula. This simple mathematical equation can be used to test your pricing and determine both the level of sales required to pay fixed costs and your Value Pay. Using the break-even formula can identify production or services volume which often relates directly to time. You can answer a critical question. *Is there enough time and where best should I allocate time?* Overall, figuring your break-even point is a great test of your proposed or existing business model.

Let's get your numbers together. I can't wait for you to see the truth: your break-even results.

Variable Costs

Variable costs are the cost basis for determining the fee or price you will charge for your products or services. Variable costs rise and fall with the volume of production or services delivered. They generally include product costs, materials, labor, delivery, packaging, and commission. They also include labor if it is paid by the volume of production or service delivery. Employees who get paid regardless of production are considered fixed costs: They get paid the same regardless of whether they do anything or not. (That's a management issue.)

Variable costs are expenses that directly relate to the production or delivery of your products and services.

When you work your DAMN Plan, you will develop management habits for regularly analyzing your variable costs.

As the boss, it is your responsibility to manage waste and get your products and services priced right to cover variable costs with enough margin to pay you your value. Here is a sample of a Variable Cost spreadsheet I use with my clients as we make determined-decisions about pricing and product or service offerings.

Variable Costs	
Raw Materials/Inventory Item	
Materials	$ 20.00
Labor	
Piecework labor	10.00
Packaging/Shipping	
Tag	1.00
Sales Commission/Staff	
Other Variable Expenses	
Total Variable Expenses	$ 31.00
Gross Profit Margin	
Value Price	$ 60.00
Minus Variable Expense	(31.00)
Equals Gross Profit Margin	$ 29.00
Gross Profit Margin Percentage	48%

Frequently, solopreneurs, consultants, coaches, and professional service providers tell me it does not cost them *anything* to deliver their services. They forget to factor in things like printed materials, sales packets, online services/app subscriptions, mileage, and other expenses directly related to serving their clients.

When I was getting my business model straightened out, I tracked my time and realized that I was driving endless hours to meet with clients. I had it in my Minnesota-nice mind that it was the best to go to where they were. I had not analyzed the cost and had not factored it into my fees, don't cha know.

Here's a quick scenario to demonstrate the problem with not knowing your numbers. Let's just say that your billable hourly rate is $100/hour. You drive fifty miles RT to meet with that client for one hour. Using the IRS deductible mileage rate of $0.575/mile times fifty miles = $28.75.

You might think that the $28.75 is a perk, a special deduction for business owners. A gift from the IRS. No. It covers real expenses to you: depreciation, car maintenance, gas, oil, tires, and insurance. If you have ever broken it down and tracked actual expenses, the IRS is NOT giving you a gift. They're simply giving you *some* credit for the investment of travel that you made into your business. So, if you have not factored in the mileage costs, not to mention the travel time and other costs, into your fee structure, you may well be losing money. For sure, you are not making $100/hour.

$$\$100 - 28.75 = \$71.25$$

If it is critical to meet on-site with your client, factor in the cost of mileage. Make a determined-decision based on the facts, not just what you think is best. My clients have grown to appreciate the efficiency of not meeting face-to-face all the time. We save and schedule in-person sessions for when being in-person matters and adds value. I help them save time and give them more value—just loading up the benefits package!

That is just one scenario. Each business is unique. Using the table below, identify variable expenses that may be incurred as you provide your services or deliver products.

In the personal budgeting exercise, we called money that trickles away "leaky money." Account for everything, right down to paper clips. You don't want leaky money in your business budget either. That's your Value Pay going down the drain. Keep track of it.

Fixed Costs

You've come a long way! You have collected most of the critical numbers you need to design a business that pays you your value.

Fixed costs are expenses that have to be paid by a company independent of any specific business activities.

Now you will review or develop your fixed cost budget, which, unlike variable costs, do not change with an increase or decrease in the volume of goods or services produced or sold. Furthermore, fixed costs are like your committed expenses in your personal budget—they must be paid regardless of sales volume or revenue coming in each month.

Fixed expenses include rent, equipment, inventory costs, marketing, payroll, insurance, and funds allocated for research and development. It is your responsibility to determine how to manage all operating costs (fixed and variable) without significantly affecting the business's ability to compete in the marketplace. It is also your responsibility to make decisions based on need rather than want.

New and old entrepreneurs sometimes are under the misguided belief that to be a "real" business, they must have the best of everything. Driven more by ego than business logic, they run out and rent a space because it is available, really nice and they will be "real." They purchase advertising—not in their marketing plan—from the inevitable ad salesperson who will find them the minute they register their business name with the state. They create and order all sorts of promotional items that sit on a shelf, never really generating sales because "real" businesses do it. Right?

No. "Real" businesses, real business managers, manage resources to maintain or increase sales. Whether you are just starting out or have been in the trenches for a while, you must check your starry eyes at the door and be logical about your spending. Here is a sample fixed cost budget worksheet. You may experience some or all of these costs in your business. You may have unique costs not shown. Identify the business needs and plan for the wants, just as you would in your personal budget.

Fixed Cost Categories	Cost
Contractual/Professional Services	
Marketing and Advertising	
Payroll and Payroll Taxes	
Banking Fees	
Entertainment	
Existing Debt Repayment	
Liability Insurance, Property, and Professional	
Internet Access and Wifi	
Lease or Rent	
Miscellaneous	
Office Supplies	
Phones, including Mobile	
Postage	
Professional Dues and Subscriptions	
Travel	
Utilities	
Other	
Other	

Other	
New Debt – Principal and Interest	
Credit Card Debt Repayment	
Personal Loan Repayment	

I know how hard it is. All those tchotchkes are so enticing. I like to use the *put it in your cart and drive it around the store for a bit* method to avoid buying stupid stuff. You may have done this, too.

Let's just say you are in Target or some big box store and a shiny object catches your attention. You think, "I could really use that! Oh, look it's even on sale—30 percent off."

With stars in your eyes, you put it in your cart, feeling great about nabbing such a good deal. Then you take your new, shiny object for a ride. As you are heading to check out, you review what you have in your cart. What do you *really* need? Toilet paper, check. Socks and underwear for the kids, check. New shiny object (which by now has lost a bit of its luster). Hmmm? No. You stick it on a shelf of kitty litter, right next to the checkout counter, pay for your needs, and triumphantly make your exit.

As you are making decisions about your fixed costs, be frugal. It's OK. It's wise and not wasteful. It's good management. Too many businesses get caught up in the image creation web, thinking that they aren't as real without all the fancy staplers, doodads, and luxury suites. Give your customers what they want—great service and *you*. Remember that people buy from people they know, like, and trust. It's just my opinion, but the days of gleaming offices seem to be making their exit stage left.

Hint: A secret to freedom, love, and money in business is to keep your fixed costs to a minimum. When you are top-heavy with fixed expenses, it's like living in a house with a hefty mortgage. You don't own the house. The house owns you.

I've identified some common fixed costs that you may incur for your business. It will be up to you to know the details of how you spend your money for operations. The best way to do this is to evaluate the past years of expenses.

Pricing And Fee Structure

Let's just get right to it. Do you know why you are charging your current fee or price? It's a bit of a loaded question; loaded with both emotion and logic.

One of my favorite topics to teach is pricing. Pricing is financial, directly affecting revenues and profitability. Pricing is management, impacting the allocation of resources, especially time. Pricing is marketing, saying so much more about you and your business than, "Here's my fee!"

With all its power and possibilities as a marketing, management, and financial tool, your price structure is one of the toughest sets of numbers to establish. It is difficult because it is more of an art than a science. It is hard to put your finger on that perfect number because pricing is riddled with emotions and the owner's core beliefs. Setting a price and owning it, heart, mind, body and soul, requires that you "get your head on straight" and believe in your value and the value of your offering.

Let's start there.

The first and best way to get your head on straight is to start seeing your business from the perspective of the consumer and the value they place on the goods and services you deliver. And the best way to remember how they might feel is to remember you are a consumer, too.

Have you ever gone shopping and picked out the perfect peaches? OMG! I love summer peaches. The warm, gooey juice dripping out both sides of your lips and down your chin when you take that first bite. Mom would buy boxes and boxes of them in the summer. We kids would sneak them and eat them around the corner of the cabin. Pretty sure she knew. Moms are like that.

Oh yeah, back to the analogy. So you've spent a good half-hour picking out your precious peaches. You've carefully placed each one, like delicate little critters, into a bag, talking to each one as you go.

"Oooo! You're a good one! Oh! Look at you! I can't wait to eat you!"

Then, some bagger at the checkout grabs them like they are rocks and you yell, "Get your hands off my peaches!" then look around and think *Did I actually say that?*

Anyway, did I ever once mention the price of peaches? No. Because I put an infinite value on a really good peach. I don't care how much they cost. The quality (value), not to mention my love for them, is greater than or equal to the price.

The guy or gal buying a brand-new Bugatti Veyron (I would like one, please!) with an 8.0-liter turbo-quad 16-cylinder engine that makes 1,000 hp and has a 200-mph-plus top speed does not haggle over price. [Insert a Tim the Toolman grunt.] The homeowner buying a really good riding lawn mower that doesn't make her butt numb after the first acre doesn't haggle over price. (I have ridden a few butt-numbing lawn mowers.) If we value what we want or need, price *may* be a consideration, but is not the first one. So quit leading with the fee your customers will pay and instead focus on value.

Your customers are more driven by outcomes, value and timely delivery than price. They may also be driven by your status and expertise. They may be driven by the convenience you offer. They may be driven by the passion you have for your work. Many factors raise or lower perceived value. So *think.* What are you *really* selling? For sure, not just any old peach. Your peaches are perfect.

By far, the most important way you can express value is by imagining your customers making an investment rather than paying a price. When you can talk about and clearly demonstrate the return on investment your clients will experience by working with you, you've struck gold.

Make it your mission to understand your clients' pain and pleasure points. (How much do they like their peaches? What do they look for in a quality peach? How many peaches are too many? How many peaches are not enough?)

Enough with the peaches. Here are some questions you can ask about the value you bring:

- If you save them time, what is the value of that time?

- If you help them improve their health, what is the value of that health improvement?

- If you save them money, how much?

- If you increase their effectiveness or productivity, how is it reflected in their bottom line?

- If you prevent them from having regrets, what is it worth to them?

- If you reduce their financial stress, what is that worth?

- If you make them look good in the eyes of their family, employer, employees, or clients, how much is that worth?

Had I known about pricing when I was so eager to start my workroom, I could have charged more for our extreme attention to detail and crazy tagline with an attitude, "If they say it can't be done, we can do it!" We took the extreme side of custom decorating, and our customers *gained clout* along with oohhs and aahhs from the crowd—as if they were suddenly driving a Bugatti—for having our designs in their homes. Not only were they custom and one-of-a-kind, but sometimes the designs seemed ridiculously impossible.

Ultimately, for our wholesale customers, *we reduced production and delivery time*. This *increased sales* overall in the studios we served, and we made the general manager *look really good*. He got to claim the success without doing the work! I had a hell of a value matrix and I didn't even know it. Damn!

It was one of those street lessons that I learned on the ground, doing my businesses. If you have been out there in the trenches, I am guessing you might have learned or are learning a few of your own lessons. No regrets! Just don't repeat them.

Not charging my value price was a mistake I will not repeat. I don't want you to make that mistake either, so your next step after exploring your customers' pain and pleasure points and calculating the value you bring will be to explore your own beliefs. To become a pricing expert, you must be able to get out of your own way.

Stop the *it feels icky* movie reel in your head.

Many of us started businesses that deliver on a close-held passion that we have. If someone asked you, "What is the work that you would do for free, if you could?" you would say, "[exactly what you do]." When your business "work" is born of this deep love, you may struggle to even think of asking someone to pay. Or you may not even recognize how what you do could be monetized.

I love working with artistic and creative people, but monetizing their creations is often a huge challenge for them. When cultural or intrinsic values embedded in their art are beyond valuation, placing a dollar value on it just feels wrong. They often feel that giving away their art is about having a giving spirit. How can you monetize the essence of who you are?

Just remember that "getting" to pay honors and increases the value in the consumer's mind. Getting to purchase allows the buyer to work with [insert your name] or they get to own a [insert your name!] Paying the right fee, the right price or making the right investment honors both you and your customer.

Lastly, free negates value. No one ever fills their bag with items from the "free" bin—even at a rummage sale!

Your first step to stop the icky pricing movie reel in your head is to recognize your own core limiting beliefs. You may or may not have some or all of these thoughts. It often depends on how you were raised, where you came from, who you have been hanging out with, and the ideas you have adopted about yourself.

The most important thing you can do right now is to recognize what you might be thinking when you say, "Your investment for [your offer and the value your customer will be receiving] is $[your price or fee]."

The list of core limiting beliefs is endless and insidious. Here are ten of a bazillion thoughts that might be affecting your ability to correctly value yourself, your products and your services:

1. I'm too old. Kids nowadays know so much more.

2. I'm too young. I don't have enough experience.

3. I'm not smart enough. I don't have a formal education.

4. That sounds greedy. Money is the root of all evil.

5. People like me don't make that kind of money. What?

6. People won't like me. The approval of others is key to my feeling worthy.

7. I'm not important.

8. I don't deserve to have more than what I have.

9. There's no point in asking for what I want. I will never get it.

10. Who do I think I am?

Your next step is to lose your fear of rejection. All I can say is, "Get a damn attitude!" You *will* be rejected. People *will* say no. You are not the only show in town. You are one of many choices. But a surefire pathway to rejection would be going into negotiations thinking that you will be turned down.

You are the *right* choice for the *right* person, business, organization, or event. You *cannot* and *should not* try to be everything to all people. Just be exactly what and who you are. Always do your best. That is enough. Don't settle. Imagine the impossible. Ask for the unlikely. Boom!

According to most academic business textbooks, there can be upward of seven Cs of pricing. That is pure evidence that pricing is an art. The seven Cs are: cost, customers, competition, compatibility, currency, culture, and channels of distribution. I have narrowed it down to cost, customers, and competition. Then I added a C of my own: Compensation—your Value Pay. Your freedom, love, and money.

Cost. This is the variable cost for each of your products or services and your fixed costs for general business operations. You must cover your cost of doing business and the cost of providing your goods and services. This is the minimum you can charge without going out of business. The only way that you can charge less is to reduce your expenses.

If you have not completed your variable and fixed cost worksheets yet, you must do it right away, or none of the rest of this will help you. To establish an accurate—staying in business—fee structure or price, you must know these numbers. No *I thinks* allowed.

Compensation. This is your Value Pay. What do you want to earn, take home, and put in your bank account? Did you do the Value Pay exercise? Do you believe in your Value Pay? If the answer is yes to both, great. If not, *go back and get your work done!* I haven't pulled the No Excuses Card for a while, so I am taking it out for a bit of exercise. You must plan to pay yourself.

Competition. Research your competitors to determine the range of prices that are charged in your industry, high to low. Then think about the perceived value that your competition brings to its customers or perhaps your customers. How does their fee structure or price align with their value?

In the art of pricing, you begin to see how you stack up against your competition. For example, if the range in the marketplace varies from $100 to $500 what value is being offered for each pricing level? How do you want to be perceived in the marketplace? Which of your competitors are most closely aligned with your value? Which of your competitors most closely resemble you or where you are going? What are they charging?

We are not talking *price competition.* Avoid competing on price like the plague. I've seen too many businesses fall into the bottomless pit of price competition. I take great care in helping my coaching clients navigate toward value pricing and away from competitive pricing.

Think about this. You can only lower prices so much before you go out of business. Meanwhile, if you do the opposite and raise prices and add value instead of lowering them and reducing value, you enter an infinite expanse. You will be like Captain Kirk on Star Trek, except infinitely more articulate.

Customers. This is your customer's perceived value of your products or services. It is what they expect to pay to get the quality they desire. It's also about your alignment with your ideal customers' wants and needs and the value they place on getting those wants and needs met. If you did not work through the questions regarding the value you bring, take a few minutes and reflect. Dig in and do some research and ask your customers about your value. What do they like about doing business with you? What value do they perceive from doing business with you?

Let's put this information together in a couple ways. First, here's a simple way of thinking about an hourly rate using your costs and compensation. This can give you a minimum pricing structure.

If you have filed taxes for your business in the past year, take a look at what you expensed. (If you are a start-up, this is still a bit of a guess. I'll give you some numbers to practice with in a moment.) Don't be afraid to make a solid guess if you don't have the exact numbers, but validate your numbers before you commit to a fee. For now, we are playing, and the numbers will get more real as you go.

In the event that you don't have your own numbers to plug in, let's assume your total expenses for a year (variable and fixed) are $60,000 and the Value Pay you desire is $75,000 per year.

Your actual numbers might be less, or they could be more. There is no judgment here. This is *your* Value Pay, not mine or anyone else's.

Let's assume you don't want to work sixty or eighty hours a week like a crazy person. Let's instead imagine a "normal" work week which equals 2,080 hours per year, or forty hours per week.

Here's the math:

$$\$60,000 + \$75,000 = \$135,000$$
$$\$135,000 \text{ divided by 2,080 hours} = \$64.90/\text{hour}$$

Now, because the IRS wants their cut and you may want to cover a few benefits, multiply that hourly rate by 1.25. This is only an estimate that may cover some benefits and pays taxes at a rate of 20 percent of wages.

$$\$64.90 \times 1.25 = \$81.13/\text{hour}$$

If you are a consultant, coach, speaker, or independent contractor, this serves *only* as a baseline. Remember three things:

1. You will not be directly billing for every hour that you work, so this is not a billable hourly rate.

2. This is still not the value of your services, nor the investment your customers will be willing to pay to work with you. It's a minimum threshold.

3. The only way that you can work for less is to pay yourself less and/or reduce your operating expenses.

This is simplistic in a way, but for our purposes right now, I want you to get started setting and believing in your price. If you can come up with your minimum, it's easy from there, so keep it simple.

Using this minimum threshold based on the costs and compensation, you can then apply the art of pricing. You can begin to adjust up from your minimum to reflect what your customers expect to pay for the value you deliver and your perceived position in the marketplace.

Here is an example:

Your research has shown that your competitive price range is $100 to $500. In your gut the $100 felt cheap even though it was more than your minimum of $81.13. You didn't trust that number. What they promised did not align with their price. This might be exactly what your customers are thinking, too. So for now let your intuition rule and say $100 is not enough.

Looking across the spectrum of your competitors, you began to see that each spoke to a different group of ideal customers. The $350-to-$500 level served an entirely different group of customers than you. They were not your ideal customers.

Reviewing your offer, the value—both intrinsic and monetary—that you offer to your ideal customers, and given your years of experience, you determine that your initial price will be $250. You feel that this fee structure reflects your position in the marketplace and your customers' expectations.

Oh, my! I know exactly what you are thinking. That's a whole pile of guts and guessing. You are not too far off in your thoughts, except that if you do your research and know your numbers you, too, will develop your Spidey senses and become very good at the art (guessing) of pricing.

The fun does not stop here. Nor will it ever stop. Pricing is not a one-and-done process. As a manager, you must constantly evaluate and change as needed. You will evaluate your initial price or fee structure and incremental increases when you do your break-even analysis. Getting your pricing right can mean the difference between having positive cash flow, being broke and flipping couch cushions. Take my word for it.

Head over to the sidebar, my friend. I would like to give you a pep talk.

Sidebar
No Excuses! You Must Know Your Numbers

Doing these exercises may have left you with a "holy buckets!" feeling. I know that some of you may have been winging it when it comes to your numbers. Others may be meticulously tracking their numbers but have never sat down with them other than to enter them into QuickBooks. They are winging it, too. So remember, you are not alone if you feel bewildered by all the numbers, research and fact finding that you must do to get your pricing right and find freedom, love, and money in your business. You are in a big group of wingers.

Regardless of where you are with your business numbers, you are here now wanting better for yourself and your business. I will say it again, it matters more where you are going and what you plan to do than where you have been and what you did. No beating yourself with a wet noodle. Decide that you will be a numbers person right now. Let me help you write a determined-decision.

To have more confidence and resolve in making my determined-decisions, I will establish an accounting system that tracks my numbers and work it regularly, using it to manage my business and stay on top of my financial position every day—not just on April 15.

There will be more on systems and management, but having an accounting system cannot be overemphasized. Knowing where your money is going is the only way you can make quality decisions. As hard as it is sometimes to face the truth of our money habits, not knowing is worse. Guessing at our financial position only creates anxiety and disrupts the focus you need to make your dreams come true.

Remember:

> *When you are broke, you can only think about money.*
>
> *When you have money, you can think about your mission.*

Whatever shape your money management systems are in, gather your numbers now. You will need to get your checkbook, credit card statements, box of bills or purse/wallet full of receipts—whatever form your spending documentation is in right now—and pull your numbers. This is about getting started *now. No excuses.* At this point, focus on getting your numbers out of your head and onto paper.

Whether this is the first time or the millionth, I want you to look at your numbers with a curious mind. No judgment. You just want the truth so you can make determined-decisions and move forward.

——————— REFLECTION ———————

How Do I See The Value Of My Offer?

#1 Truth. How am I feeling about my competition and what they charge compared to my pricing structure?

_____

_____

_____

#2 Truth. Am I experiencing a bit of _Who do you think you are?_ Why?

_____

_____

_____

#3 Truth. Is what I am telling myself about the value of my services/products based on fact or past stinking thinking?

_____

_____

_____

#4 Truth. What's my image of a real business owner in my field? Do I see myself in that image? If not, why?

_____

_____

_____

#5 Truth. Do I think others see me as a real business owner? How much does this matter to me?

_____

_____

_____

#6 Truth. What is the value of my offer? What do my clients receive from investing in my products or services?

_____

_____

_____

When a business only has the capacity to make you $10, it does not matter how much harder you work—the most you will make is $10.

Step Five: Breakeven = Confident Determined-Decisions

When a business only has the capacity to make you $10, it does not matter how much harder you work—the most you will make is $10. That is a cold, hard truth. Way too many entrepreneurs fall into the trap of thinking that they can squeeze blood from a turnip and somehow find themselves pocketing more than their particular business is capable of earning. I believe you are on a more enlightened path than those starry-eyed entrepreneurs, if only because you have the DAMN book in your hands. You want different. You want to earn more and actually work less than you do right now. *Right?*

Do not be one of the 84 percent flying by the seat of their pants, putting out fires, and making knee-jerk decisions. You can do better.

When you master this new way of being, this new habit, believe it or not you will truly become a DAMN Planner with a damn fine, confident attitude.

Breakeven is the point at which your business covers all variable and operating costs and meets your personal financial requirements.

I had already run two businesses before I had ever heard of breakeven. Some days, I think I did things backward. I went to college and majored in English and theater arts, then started businesses. Then after my street learning, I went back to college to get my business degrees, *then* decided to start writing. Weird, right?

Actually, by the time I went back to college with my attitude intact, I was ready to learn the theories and technical tools of business. Prior to that, I may have been like some of my clients, so busy working in their businesses that they can't pay attention. It happens.

In the introduction, I mentioned that I wanted to save you some pain. Well, here is where the rubber meets the road: breakeven. No matter how you twist your business story with words, the numbers will tell the true story and breakeven means just what it says. Breakeven is the point at which your business covers all variable and operating costs and meets your personal financial requirements. Your business is at zero profit at breakeven, and it is where loss ends and profits begin to accumulate. This is the point at which your business, product, or project becomes financially viable.

Breakeven is your new measuring stick for analyzing your business decisions by the numbers, including how to get paid your value. Breakeven provides significant insight into the level of sales necessary to cover your business's expenses, including the cost of employing *you*.

I want you to take this exercise very seriously. If you didn't just make up the numbers instead of taking the time to gather them, breakeven won't lie. I have hammered home the importance of knowing your numbers, but I also really want you to learn to play—yup, play! This is about testing different business designs with different operating costs and pricing structures. You can shift and focus on a different ideal customer who will pay more, or you can choose to serve a larger target market at a lower cost, going the volume sales route. The choices are yours. This is the beginning that may open doors you never even knew were there.

A recent DAMN Plan workshop participant shared an epiphany after running through a quick break-even exercise.

"Oh my gosh! I have customers from when I first started (and I was hungry) who are paying me half of what my current clients are paying, and they are taking 80 percent of my time."

She went on to calculate the change in revenue if she flipped that equation and 80 percent of her time was devoted to working with full-value clients. Damn!

Another client, in love with her signature product, did not believe me when I said that I thought her "signature" product was keeping her broke. We set up various scenarios, estimating the volume of sales she thought she would like to have for each product line. Then I asked her how many of her favorites she *thought* she could sell. Of course, she said if she just sold more than she did last year (like triple) of her signature product, she would be fine.

Well, she was wrong! In fact, when she took her signature product out of the equation, she was immediately profitable, for one simple reason. For every one of her signature products that she produced and delivered, she was losing $250.

What do you think she did with this information? First, she shed a few tears, and then she said, "Bye, Felicia!" The numbers don't lie, but it's heartbreaking to find out your favorite product or service is breaking the bank.

I've had my moments; you may have them as well. We all fall in love with certain clients or products. From my experience, breakeven is the best breakup tool ever. It's also a great way to sort through the pile of potential lovers (products, ideas, and various other opportunities). It's better than Match.com!

Breakeven is an essential tool for testing a variety of business design scenarios. It is your gateway to finding your right-fit business. Not the one that looks like someone else's or is designed in a way you heard it should be.

You left your day job to express yourself, your ideas, and your style. This is your business; your journey starts with *What if . . . ?* and your imagination. Breakeven *will* validate your assumptions so you can decide to implement—or not—and be confident in your decision.

Right now, you have my full permission to *play with the numbers*. Please, please learn to play. This is all about finding love, money and freedom in your business. If you are looking for issues and problems, you will only see issues and problems. If you are looking for opportunities and possibilities with a creative, open mind, you will find more opportunities and possibilities than you have ever imagined.

You have not come this far to only come this far. You have done the hard work of gathering your numbers—even that leaky money—to determine your fixed and variable costs. You have set your Value Pay as the owner and made initial decisions about your business's fee/price structure.

This "magic" formula will help you figure out how many units of your product or service you need to sell to break even. Let the playful calculating begin!

Number of Units to Break Even

(fixed costs + your Value Pay)
divided by
(sales price per unit—variable costs per unit)

$5,000 per month (fixed costs) + $6,000 per month (Value Pay)
divided by

$100 per hour (sales price per unit) - $28.75 (variable cost per unit)
equals

$11,000/$71.25 = *154.4 billable hours monthly to break even*

If a consultant wants to work forty hours per week and works 4.33 weeks per month, they have 173.2 total working hours per month. Is it logical that one consultant could bill out 154.4 hours every month?

It might be, if they are eating on the fly and peeing in a cup under their desk, with just over forty-five minutes to spare each day. That is not logical. This consultant needs to go get a job.

Let's play with the numbers and see if we can figure out a DAMN Plan that will keep this consultant building their dream.

Let's bump the hourly rate by $25 and reduce fixed costs by $1,000. We are just playing for now. As DAMN Planners we would validate these assumptions with research, facts, and numbers. Now our equation looks like this.

$$\$10,000/\$96.25 = \textit{104 billable hours to break even}$$

Now can it be done? Well, at least they have time to go to the bathroom, get some marketing done, and work on their business if they only need to bill out twenty-four hours per week instead of the thirty-six hours in the first scenario.

I can hear the hecklers in the audience.

It's just on paper! It's easy when you are just working it out on paper.

Me (with my damn attitude): "Yes, it is. It's much better than working it out on the street and going broke."

You might also ask whether it is realistic to think that operating costs could be cut by $1,000 per month. Here are some ideas on how you can cut your operational expenses:

- Choose to cowork or establish a home office instead of renting a private office for $1,000.

- Build relationships and boost sales by contacting two to three people per day via email, phone calls, or texts and save $1,000/month on paid ads.

- Contract with a virtual assistant for $1,000 per month rather than paying an employee $15/hour, thirty hours a week ($1,948.50) to sit at a front desk.

The decisions are yours. Make your determined-decisions by the numbers.

I know you're also wondering how realistic it is to think you could charge $25 dollars more per hour.

The likelihood that you can make this happen really depends on your belief in your offer, the value you are bringing to your clients and whether or not you are working with your ideal clients, the ones who value your offer.

Remember I told you I increased revenues five-fold in two years. I did it by managing my time and getting my value straight (mostly in my head). So yes, I believe raising your rates $25/hour is doable in some markets, especially if you are already grossly undervaluing yourself and your offer.

I was providing incredible value to my clients, offering business/strategic planning and fundraising services. For every dollar they were paying me, I generated $25. Not bad, huh? Really good for them. Not so good for me, but it was all my fault.

My head was thinking, *take what you can get. Don't rock the boat. This is a pretty secure thing you've got going here.*

Pretty secure, all right! I was anchored to the bottom and digging deeper every hour I worked. So I started raising my fees. Holy buckets, I was scared. I'm not going to lie. By the end of the two-year period, I had raised my prices 300 percent, and no one batted an eyelash. No one blinked. Damn!

All I really needed to do was believe, then get my damn attitude on and *show* (not just *think* they should know) my clients my value in facts and numbers. It was indisputable. I was worth their investment!

Are you ready to play with your own numbers and see what changes you can make? I hope so—you are damn well worth it!

Now that we have looked at units sold to break even, let's take a quick look at the sales volume you'll need. The break-even formula looks like this:

Break-Even Sales Volume

fixed costs + your Value Pay
divided by
(contribution margin/price)

This time let's say you are selling a pillow for $100 (price) and it costs $45 (variable cost) to produce. In this case for every pillow sold, $55 is generated to pay the fixed costs plus the owner's Value Pay. The $55 is called the contribution margin because each $55 contributes toward paying fixed costs and the owner's Value Pay. The math is simple.

Contribution Margin Equals Price
Minus Variable Cost

Imagine this is a small workroom—a one-woman shop working out of her living room. She is just getting started and pricing is a total guessing game for her. I wonder where I came up with this scenario. Hehe!

Let's just say these are very expensive, total foo-foo pillows and it takes this one-woman show forty-five minutes to make each one. Her break-even equation looks like this.

$5,000 per month (fixed costs) + $6,000 per month (Value Pay)

divided by

$55 (contribution margin)/$100 (price)

equals

$11,000/55% (contribution margin)

equals

$20,000 sales or 200 pillows at $100 each

That's 200 pillows x 45 minutes = 9,000 minutes or 150 hours per month. OMG! Here we go again.

Can it be done? Yes and no. It really depends how many hours per week she wants to work. Back in the day when I was twenty-four years old with more stamina than brains, yes, I could do it. But at what cost? I had a baby. One of the reasons I quit my day job was to be at home with my child. Guess what? I had to send her to daycare so I could stay home and work. Now that is just illogical. I was totally winging it!

Let's do the Superwoman thing and spin the world backward to reverse time. What should our woman do? Raise her prices? Reduce her variable costs? Sew faster and improve productivity? Yes, yes, and yes.

Let's just say that she finds a less expensive vendor for materials and reduces her variable costs by $10 per pillow. Then she raises her price by $5. That is reasonable, and her customers probably won't even blink, because her pillows are just that cool.

Oh, and she gets her butt out of the living room (a totally nonproductive environment) and rents a small space with better tables where she can really rock and roll. No more dancing around Legos, Weebles and blanket forts.

Her fixed costs go up by $750 per month for the space. Her variable costs are now down to $35 per pillow, and her price is $105 per pillow. Her contribution margin is now $105 minus $35 which equals $70. The move increases her productivity. She can now whip out a pillow in thirty minutes, so she reduced her time per pillow by 33 percent.

Can't wait to see how this works out, can you? Me, neither.

$5,750 per month (fixed costs) + $6,000 per month (Value Pay)

divided by

$70 (contribution margin)/$105 (price)

equals

$11,750/.67 (67% contribution margin)

equals

$17,537 sales or 167 pillows at $105 each

With her new, high-speed, undistracted productivity model, she now only has to work eighty-four hours a month to hit breakeven. Baby still goes to daycare, but not from morning until night. She also now has time to work on her business and build her dream.

This is highly simplified, but I want more than anything to show you how the numbers can help you make determined-decisions with confidence. I wish I had known this stuff back then. No regrets, though. Now that I know better, I do better in so many ways. You can, too.

Breakeven = Confident Determined-Decisions

For the sake of clarity, I have kept the scenarios simple, with one-woman shops and single products, but the same line of thinking applies regardless of the size or complexity of the business. If you have ten employees and fifteen products, it's still about the numbers. If you are operating a Main Street storefront with high overhead and buying your products wholesale, it's still about the numbers. If you are a solopreneur running your business out of the back bedroom, it's still about the numbers.

The break-even formula is still the same. Time and money are resources you must have in order for your business—and yourself—to survive, let alone thrive! It is your job to know how much you need.

Your turn. It's time to play with *your* numbers.

You can crunch your numbers manually on a piece of paper using the calculator on your phone, or right here in this book. This really isn't rocket science.

To start, you need to have the following numbers ready to plug and play:

1. Your Value Pay

2. Your variable costs

3. Your fixed costs

4. Your value price/fee structure

These might be all in the form of assumptions, wishes, or desires right now. Or you may be pulling hard-core, real numbers from your existing business's financials. Either way, it's all about challenging yourself and experimenting to see how some minor adjustments can result in a major impact on your bottom line.

Now let's get this party started! I know this might not seem like fun to you, but what can I say? I just love this stuff.

Number Of Units To Break Even

(fixed costs + your Value Pay)
divided by
(sales price per unit—variable costs per unit)

```
```

Break-Even Sales Volume

fixed costs + your Value Pay
divided by
(contribution margin/price)

```
```

In our play scenarios, I asked some basic questions about time because it is the one absolute. You cannot manufacture more time. You can change systems and business models but there are still only twenty-four hours in a day. As you play with your numbers visualize the transactions happening or products being produced. Ask yourself, can this be done? Is there enough time? What needs to change to make this work? Do I need new clients? Do I need to change my offer? Do I need to discipline myself to act consistently without distraction?

The questions are endless, and they never stop. The minute you quit asking the two most important questions in business is the day you are sunk.

How are we doing?

What can we do better?

To further translate what you are seeing in your break-even analysis, you will want to consider each and every assumption you made in your budgets, cost projections and pricing model.

- Personal budget

- Value Pay

- Time budget

- Value price

- Operating costs

- Variable costs

Do a reality check. Go through all your numbers with a fine-toothed comb. Look for places to cut or modify. Most importantly, validate your assumptions with sound market research.

There is no limit to how many times you can change your original assumptions and run your break-even analysis again. Bump your price up and down. Imagine working in a different location, with different clients, and fewer expenses. Then ask yourself more questions.

From a personal financial perspective, ask:

To build the business I have in mind, can I cut expenses in my personal budget?

Can I take on a side hustle for a short period of time?

Can someone pitch in a bit more to help?

What is my timeline for reaching my Value Pay rate?

From the perspective of precious time allocation, ask:

Is the time I have to allocate for business enough to deliver my product or service and run (work on) my business?

Can I allocate more time? Am I willing to sacrifice whatever I'm currently doing in order to meet my goals?

Is hiring or contracting for help an option?

What is the extra cost—in the form of both time and money—if I hire or contract for help? Do I want to supervise others?

Do I work well with others?

From the perspective of your customers, ask:

Who are the people or businesses that would pay for my product or service? Do I want to work with them? If not, why? If so, how?

Are there enough people to buy my product or service in the market I serve? If not, can or would I move to a new market? If so, what will it take to enter that market? What are the barriers to entry?

How will I get the attention of this new market or increase my market share where I am currently?

Do I have the time to engage in a more robust marketing plan? How can I amp up or be more consistent about my current marketing activities?

From the management cost control perspective, ask:

Are the products or services that I am selling costing me more to deliver than I am charging?

Can I cut unnecessary fixed expenses?

Can I reduce variable costs?

Be inquisitive. Trust your gut. Use your research. This is not the time to say, "Well, this is how everyone does it," or "This is just the way it is," or "There is nothing I can do about that."

DAMN Planners don't just think outside the box, they kick out the sides. Test different scenarios. What if you raised your prices? What if you gave up your lease space and worked virtually? What if you laid someone off? What if you let a few high-cost/low-value clients go? What if . . .

This is your time to shine. You are authorized and responsible. You are the boss. This is how you make your determined-decisions—by the numbers. In the end, confidence will come from knowing that your business can be done. You will be able to see what must be done to make it work—no guessing or *I think*. With shoulders back and head held high, attitude intact you will move forward with resolve.

I mentioned being able to visualize earlier. Visualization is an important technique to learn for building confidence. So head over to the sidebar. I want you to start visualizing—

believing in your head—that you can do what you always said you would.

Sidebar
Visualize Your Determined-Decisions

I know that I told you to stop "just thinking" and know your numbers, but I need to make a huge exception. I want you to think at a higher level and visualize your determined-decisions in action. I want you to imagine yourself consistently acting on your determined-decisions. I want you to see the people who are with you. I want you to see yourself enjoying freedom, love, and money. I want you to want it so bad that the idea of quitting makes you ill.

Star athletes, dancers, and performers visualize their every move prior to a competition or performance. I raised a visualizer, one of those kids that just can see and then do. This is the same kid who gave me bad knees and prayer holes in my jeans.

I bought him a snowboard when he was nine. As I inquired at the lodge about lessons, someone poked me in the shoulder. "Isn't that Sean?" I turned to see my son gliding down the advanced hill and launching into a 360. I scrambled to the bottom of the hill, prepared to put pieces back together. He slid up next to me like a pro, all smiles and chest puffed out.

"Who taught you to do that?" I squeaked through breaths as my mother-heart leapt in my bosom.

"I watched the other guys and just did it," he responded nonchalantly, insinuating that he didn't know what I was so worked up about.

Three years later, he built a steam engine that, by all engineering standards, shouldn't have worked. But it did. By sixteen, he had advanced to making cars go too fast by fabricating fuel systems from what he could scrounge up or buy from Ace Hardware. Enough said on that topic, other than to impart a simple moral: What we think matters. Our beliefs and the pictures we put in our heads matter. If you think you can or can't, you are right either way.

Visualization is one of the best ways to bring resolve to your determined-decisions. When we can see it on paper and then visualize it, the results become real. When you work through the following exercise, take note of how your business fits (or doesn't) within the context of your life. How are you feeling? What are you believing? Are there core limiting beliefs creeping in?

The very first time I shared this exercise, I had a room full of women, all relaxed with their eyes closed, walking through daily operations in their minds, mixing what had to be done in their businesses with their very real lives.

One of the women yelped, "Well, damn! I have just designed a business identical to the job I am leaving. I hate it!" Holy buckets!

Another woman imagined her very energetic two-year-old grabbing her cell phone and accidently calling her best client. Holy buckets!

Many breathed a sigh of relief, seeing a less-stressful and well-defined business where they closed the doors of their offices and focused on ideal clients who were delighted to invest in the outcomes they delivered. Happy dance!

As my clients have walked through the visualization exercise with me, there have been some serious *Happy dance!* moments and some outrageous *Holy buckets!* moments.

If your visualization exercise reveals a "holy buckets!" moment, just say, "Here's your sign." Make a U-turn and map out your revised plan to take you straight to *your* right-fit destination. Do not settle for less. You have the tools to tweak your DAMN Plan to fit your *actual* lifestyle, not the fictitious examples or idealistic ones based on other people's values and responsibilities.

Visualization Exercise

First, find a safe, comfy space to do this exercise where you are not distracted. Even kick the cat out of the room. You can increase the effectiveness of this exercise by having someone read you the following questions:

- It's time to get ready for your day. What time is it? You get dressed for work. What do you wear?

- Someone depends on you for something before you start your workday. Who is it? What do they need?

- You "open the doors" of your business. What does it look like? Where are you?

- Who else is with you?

- You develop, produce, or handle the product or service of your business. What is it?

- You interact with a client/customer. What do they really want or need? Why have they come to you? How did they find you? Think deeply about who they are by drawing a mental picture.

- Was there a sales transaction? How will you get paid? Will they be back? How often?

- It's time for a break or lunch. Where did you eat? With whom? What did you eat?

- What does the second half of your day look like? Maybe it's one steady stream. Ask yourself, "Who is in control of my day?"

- It's time to call it a day. What time is it? Does your day ever end?

- You review your finances, do your books and look at financial transactions. How much did you earn? How much is actual cash in your hand? How much is owed? When and how will you get paid? Do you do your own bookkeeping?

- Where have you been working? Maybe you are home. Do you shut a door behind you to close up for the day? If you aren't at home, do you go straight there after work? What does your workspace look like when you leave it for the day?

- When you decide to be done, what time is it? Do you have personal responsibilities that must be managed right away? Do you have time to play and enjoy? Are you feeling like you should just keep working?

- You talk to someone about your day. Who do you talk to?

- You need to prepare for tomorrow. What do you do? When do you do it?

- It's time to sleep. What time is it?

Now, open your eyes and answer these questions.

1. When you visualize your business, what is the best part? If you could do more of this (or do it all the time), would you?

2. When you visualized your business, was there a part that zapped your energy? Why? How can you change the scenario to reduce the suckiness?

3. Were the human interactions in your business rewarding for you, your associates, and your customers?

4. Were there others in the picture who either added to or diminished the positive energy in your day? How can you approach them or the scenario differently to change the outcome?

5. Can you see yourself achieving the sales numbers reflected in your break-even analysis? If so, what does it feel like? If not, what are your concerns, doubts, fears? Why do you feel this way?

There is nothing wrong with trusting these visceral feelings. Your gut is a good predictor. Step away from the numbers. Take some time to visualize. Talk to a trusted guide. Then come back to this reflection exercise.

How will this business model change your life? Who will be impacted? How will they respond?

It sounds great to say you want to or can make $1 million, but are you willing to do what it takes to make $1 million? If not, why? If so, how?

—————— REFLECTION ——————

What If You Made Changes To Your Business?

#1 Truth. What scares me most about making changes to my business? Why?

_____

_____

_____

#2 Truth. What excites me most about making changes to my business? Why?

_____

_____

_____

#3 Truth. Who can I share my thoughts, ideas, and determined-decisions with? Who will kick my backside with love so I make necessary changes and stay resolved?

_____

_____

_____

"Would you tell me, please, which way I ought to go from here?" asked Alice.

"That depends a good deal on where you want to get to," said the cat.

"I don't much care where—" said Alice.

"Then it doesn't matter which way you go," said the cat.

"—so long as I get SOMEWHERE," Alice added as an explanation.

"Oh, you're sure to do that," said the cat, "if you only walk long enough."

—Lewis Carroll, *Alice in Wonderland*

4

A Is For Act Consistently

I would have done well as Alice in Wonderland. I relish going on undetermined, unscheduled travel adventures. Unstructured time to refresh my spirit is good for my roaming soul. I encourage my coaching clients to take time to fill their gas tanks, too, but remind them that wandering (a.k.a. winging it) doesn't work so well in business.

If Alice had asked for business guidance and direction, it might have created an interesting plot twist for the Cheshire Cat to say, "Follow me! I have the DAMN Plan."

All snarky cattiness aside, every venture begins with a plan and two simple questions: Where are you *right now*? Where do you *want to go*? It is impossible to plan a trip, a birthday party, or a business if you don't know your starting point or where you are going.

To paraphrase the Cheshire Cat and take it a step further, "If you don't know where you are going, any road will get you there *and* if you never take action, you get to stay right where you are."

My heart breaks when would-be entrepreneurs sit, ruminate, plan, worry, go 'round and 'round in great discussions at an endless tea party with the Mad Hatter. They just can't seem to get off the dime.

Years ago, I used *turning ideas into action* as one of my taglines. This isn't just some catchphrase or an expression of my love for ideas. It is serious.

Nothing happens until you act.

Moreover, you will not act or make the necessary changes until the pain of staying exactly where you are is greater than the pain or challenge of moving forward. Yes, there is risk in taking action. You could be right. You could be wrong. *Some decisions will be better than others, but in the end, we are built by actions taken—not by the time spent on the sidelines.*

You will never know if your ideas, decisions, or your pricing are right until you act. Your only proof, the only real validation of all your assumptions is if someone actually agrees to invest in your services or products. Putting the check in the bank is nice, too!

But not all actions are created equal. There is busy-ness and then there is business. There are actions that you take every once in a while, and then there are consistent actions.

To realize the freedom, love, and money you seek in your business, your actions must be intentional and consistent. In other words, your actions must meet the following criteria.

1. They are aligned with your priorities.

2. They are in alignment with your goals.

3. They have a measurable outcome.

4. You will take the actions regardless of conditions or feelings. No excuses.

The actions you take every day will correlate directly with the outcomes you achieve. If you spend inordinate amounts of time watching reruns on Netflix, you will know a lot about old television shows. If you act according to your priorities with full knowledge of what you expect to achieve, you will build confidence. Action builds confidence. Confidence builds resilience. Resilience is the hallmark of the successful.

I have lost time, money, and relationships by not aligning my actions with my priorities. No regrets. No wallowing in what could have been. The only time we fail is when we do not learn from those life events or past mistakes and let them hold us down.

Today is a new day. It's a good day to plant some new habits and do what you always said you would do.

Everything you have learned up to this point has value. But it will not mean a damn thing or make any difference in your life or someone else's unless you act on it. You've expressed your willingness. You have located your kickass motivator. You are resolved and have visualized some of your first determined-decisions.

Now is the time to act.

However small your initial actions may be, taking action—putting yourself out there even when you are scared—is not only courageous, it will also dissolve the fear. Let me say it again, every action you take, regardless of the outcome, will fortify your *confidence* and hone *resilience*. These are two character traits that you'll need to push yourself to new heights;

to keep going when the going gets tough and you need to make a comeback.

I have been sharing the story of my workroom here and there in this book. Yes, I got lucky in the first year and did end up parlaying my entrepreneurial heat into a tidy little business that paid me my value and gave me some freedom, love, and money. But the part of the story that "built me" has nothing and everything to do with what it takes to make it as a business owner.

I was pregnant. After two miscarriages, I was half scared and half happy. My clients were excited. They assured me that they would work with me no matter what.

Well, "no matter what" happened. My water broke in the fifth month. I was put on bed rest. I had two options. I could stay in the hospital or if I could "be a very good girl and stay in bed," I could go home.

It's amazing the thoughts that plow through your head. Some make you cry, some make you ashamed, and some make you sick. If I didn't work, if I let the business die, we would lose everything. If I didn't quit, I would run the risk of killing my baby. Damn it! Damn it all, anyway!

Believe it or not, I moved my business back into the living room and made the roll-out couch my bedroom. I hired an assistant. I kept the business parade going as best I could. Even the general manager that I made look so good came to see me in my new "office."

I limped along until I went into labor for real. My daughter, Michelle, born in the seventh month, was three pounds and four ounces with a quirky smile. By the time she was four months old, she'd had four surgeries. Days, I worked. Nights, my four-year-old and I stayed in the NICU with Michelle. I was running on attitude, a fighter's spirit, and fear.

Just short of her six-month birthday, my little fighter couldn't fight anymore. Knowing her struggle, I was again half happy, and this time, totally broken.

As we celebrated her life and laid her to rest, the bills started to arrive in brown manilla envelopes. Let's just say, when you get medical bills in manilla envelopes and you have exhausted your insurance, you can just bend over and kiss your backside goodbye.

It's a bit of a blur, but before it was over, I was curled up in the last chair in the house, waiting for the banker to come and get the keys.

"Nothing worse can happen," I told my friend. "If this isn't the bottom, I can sure see it from here."

We joked about bottom bouncing and getting blood out of a turnip. No real feelings came out. To speak the truth would have been too painful. The mailman came up the walk and handed me three more brown manilla envelopes. This time from the IRS.

You couldn't make this up. The IRS was auditing me for three years running.

"Screw that. It can get worse."

Never—*never* did I imagine this as part of my life. Did I see it coming? Yes. Could I have kept it from happening? No.

The reality is, there are events outside our control. Despite our belief that somehow we can control everything, we only have the power to control our response, and hope is not a strategy.

When it all seems impossible, even with the fear and pain you might be experiencing, *you must act.* Action is the cure.

Your first action is asking for and accepting help.

When I was actually open to receive, my help came from an unexpected place. One of the nurses at the NICU was engaged to be married, and everyone was telling her that her ideas and designs for her wedding party couldn't be done. She didn't want to settle, so she asked if I could make her wedding dress, five bridesmaid's dresses, two flower girl dresses and a matching wedding dress for a porcelain doll.

I said, "Sure! They say it can't be done? I can do it!"

Heck, I had studied theatrical costume design in college. I had made clown costumes, even a giant corn-on-the-cob suit to open a chain of popcorn stands. I had sewn tutus for the North Dakota Ballet and designed the donkey costume for Shakespeare's *Midsummer Night's Dream*. Wedding dresses? Why not?

That nurse thought I was helping *her*, but her small request got my mind off all the things going wrong and the failure I thought I'd become. It got me started again. When I quit thinking that this new start was small and that I was now small, I saw the real opportunity in front of me. I started a side hustle designing clothes for hard-to-fit people, including brides, who are notoriously hard to fit.

I called it The Eye of the Needle (an homage to *Eye of the Tiger* and Sylvester Stallone.) My tagline was, "If they say it can't be done, I can do it!"

I tell you this story because, as I have already said, you will operate your business in the midst of your very real life. There will be events and people outside your control. There will be times when you just want to curl up in your chair and feel sorry for yourself forever. There will be times when you feel like you absolutely cannot take another step.

Sometimes it's fear that your plans won't work out. Sometimes you are worried about what other people think. Sometimes you can't take one more rejection. Sometimes it feels as if the entire world (and your family) is conspiring against you. Sometimes you are trying so damn hard and nothing is happening. It's real.

I will never tell you to "just get over it" as some of the most important people in my life suggested I should get over my grief for my daughter.

Instead, I am telling you, "Don't let it stop you!"

Admit your frustrations. Admit to your fears. Admit that you are tired. Then figure out what your next step is and take it. You can if you believe you can. It could be as simple as a to-do list.

Can I get a show of hands for to-do list makers? How about "I gotta remember to do this" sticky note takers? How about the people who write themselves a sticky note to remind themselves to look at their to-do list? Did you really just put up your hand?

My little-big sister's list-making habits are the stuff of legend. I think Craig Bruce, podcast host and author, had her number when he said, "My to-do list is so long that it doesn't have an end; it has an event horizon."

If you can't laugh about some things, you will drive yourself to distraction, and we can't have that. You need to stay focused.

My little-big sister, Sharie, is an extraordinary planner and she does have lists down to a simple science that she has implemented successfully since we were kids.

Being the middle kid of seven, she was sort of a Cinderella, and there would be no going to the "ball" if the house didn't get cleaned. I am not going to go into what it meant to clean the house when we were kids, but let's just say we have dusted our fair share of baseboards and cleaned behind stoves. Nowadays, my sister just buys a new house when it's time to dust the baseboards. OK, that's a joke! Not really, though. She's on house number eight.

Here's her step-by-step process for getting a house cleaned or anything done. Getting the house cleaned by noon was the goal—the expected outcome. (Step One: What's the goal— what do you expect as a result of your actions?)

Then she decided what had to be done. (Step Two: What actions must be taken?) The tasks were dusting, vacuuming, changing bedding, scrubbing toilets, cleaning the stove and fridge, and wiping those damn baseboards. There was no Cinderella-style floor scrubbing. This was the 1970s and kitchen carpet was all the rage! Gross.

My sister assembled her team. (Step Three: Who is responsible for getting the actions done?) No fairy godmother. No mice or obnoxious, tweeting birds. Just me! A master of delegation, my sister divided the list according to which of us was faster or more capable for each task. (Step Four: Match skills with the tasks to be done. Later we will talk about the fact that you, the owner, might not be the best person for the job.) Let's get real. I think I was assigned what she didn't want to do. She was the big sister; the manager of resources. She was the boss!

Off we went with our lists and tools in hand, dead set on getting out of the house by noon. (Step Five: Set a deadline and know how long it will really take to do your tasks.) Keeping in the good graces of Mom and my sister's social life depended on our planning and performance. (Step Six: Plan to be successful.)

Sounds simple, right?

The hardest part is starting. Getting your backside out of bed, or pried loose from other distractions and then doing what you said you would—consistently. This is precisely why I talked about time habits, willingness, and focus first. This is all up to you. Sharie could help you, but you can't have her—she's mine.

The DAMN Plan way of making a to-do list is a simple strategy like my little-big sister's list; you break down your action plan into specific, doable tasks that can get done in a *specific short period of time*. Each task is directly related to one of your determined-decisions or goals. I recommend that you focus on one goal at a time.

We begin with the expected outcome of your work. Let's say you have made the determined-decision that you need a website and would like to get it launched in ninety days. First, do some research to see if your timeline is realistic. Being realistic is a key factor for the success of your action plan.

No Excuses Card time! Just a mild admonition: *Do not say you can do something in two days if it's going to take a week.* That's just setting yourself up for failure. No confidence gained there.

In this case, the answer to "How long will it take?" depends on whether you are using a professional web designer or putting up a quick site with a website builder. It is mostly dependent on how much *actual* time you can devote to development. If you are fully booked with client work for the next three months, it would be unlikely you have enough time (or brain cells) left to write the content.

For every task you write on your to-do list, ask yourself how long it will take to complete. Then add up the total hours you have committed for yourself or others. You can't go over your twenty-four hour daily limit. Being realistic and honest with yourself about how much time you have, how much time you can commit, and how long it *actually* takes to complete a task is a critical step to ensure the successful completion of your action plan.

One more thing before we leave the topic of time. The time devoted to each task is the amount of time you could realistically get the task done, *if* there were no distractions. As you set your due dates, you will also factor in life, time gremlins, and ongoing work that must get done. In other words, life and business will go on.

This is an "I will" list, not an "I might" list. I want you to be successful, so I want you to be realistic. If you consistently overbook your time, you will always be disappointed in your performance. To create confidence and momentum, your actions must produce outcomes in the timeframe you *believe* they should. Our minds are like that.

Now that you have established a realistic timeline for getting your website built, identify the individual tasks that can be done within a specific period of time and who can do them.

Beyond allocating time, your action plan needs to also allocate financial resources. Your best intentions can get sabotaged by no money in the bank account. Damn! For each task that has a monetary cost, include that dollar figure in your action plan. This dollar figure must also be included in your budget. Then you must designate the funds, raise the funds, or save the funds.

However you cover the cost, obtaining the funds becomes a new task. If you must raise or save the funds before certain tasks can be done, you may need to adjust your timeline. Here is how "getting your website done" might look as an action plan:

Outcome: New website published in 90 days		Time Period: Week One			
Date	Task	Time	Who	Done By	Cost
Today	Find web designer	3 hours	You	mm/dd	$$
Day 2	Pick websites for swipe file; send to designer	2 hours	You	mm/dd	
Day 3	Send designer all current branding media	1 hour	You	mm/dd	
Day 4	Complete web designer's guide	3 hours	You	mm/dd	
Day 5	Write content for About page	3 hours	You	mm/dd	
Day 6	Find a photographer for photo shoot	2 hours	You	mm/dd	$$
Day 6	Write product/service descriptions	5 hours	You	mm/dd	
Total Time Devoted		**19 hours**			

Give your action plan a reality check. Do you have nineteen hours available? If the total number of hours you have committed—along with finishing your *regular* work—is greater than the hours you can devote, move tasks to the next week, delegate or outsource.

There is a tendency to think we are superhuman, with unlimited time and perfect lives within which the unexpected never happens. Everything doesn't have to get done today. Do what you can today. Do the next task tomorrow. You are building a new habit of taking consistently focused action, not doing a one-time big push.

That is how you get a job done The DAMN Plan way. Now let's talk about procrastination and nonnegotiable tasks that you must get done every day.

I am a professional procrastinator. I belong to Procrastinators Anonymous. I will pay the dues tomorrow. That's a joke! But procrastination is not. It is an insidious habit. In the past I could delay doing just about anything and it showed in so many ways: stress, lost income, poor personal and business relationships, and more.

I struggled with all the causes of procrastination: fear, perfectionism, too many focuses, and lack of motivation. I kicked the procrastination habit by locating my kickass motivator that kept me focused. I moved past perfectionism by aligning myself with people who held me to my deadlines which prevented me from perfecting to the nth degree.

The other way that I got past the procrastination problem was to narrow down my to-do list or action plan to be no more than three nonnegotiable tasks to get done on any one given day.

I call them nonnegotiable because that is what they are. Here is the simple rule that I have established for myself.

I cannot quit until I am done.

This has reinforced another important rule of business. Don't bite off more than you can chew even if you do have tiger teeth. That, my friend, was the root of my procrastination problem. I thought I was Superwoman and simply took on more than I could do. Then, looking at the pile of work, I would get overwhelmed. If you are overwhelmed, you will procrastinate. If you procrastinate you will underperform.

So here is my damn simple plan—my Sharie plan. I use a sticky note. I look over my big plans and pull no more than three (some days only one) items that I will get done that day. Whatever I choose, it is labeled nonnegotiable. I chain myself, mentally, to just those items. Like in the action plan scenario, I only commit to what I know I can get done within the time I have.

It's amazing how good it feels when you take a marker and aggressively scratch off each item. I love my nonnegotiables.

They work because you can see the work getting done. There is nothing worse than feeling like there is no end—like your to-do list has an event horizon. It will zap your motivation in a heartbeat. Then you are right back to procrastinating because the task is too big. I love the little buzz of success in my head. I dance around the office. I feel accomplished and ready for more. So if you struggle with procrastination, kick it with nonnegotiables.

Two more action items to talk about before we move on to minding your business; these are wash, rinse, and repeat everyday tasks. Making a habit of doing these two things consistently, every morning, has given me confidence. These two tasks combined do not take more than an hour per day. That is a small investment of time for the return.

1. Take a quick review of your financial position. For me, this means keeping my QuickBooks up to date.

2. Make two to three marketing contacts with past, present, and future clients. For me, this means making a phone call, texting, or sending an email simply intended to build a relationship. Sometimes, it means sending out a handwritten note.

One step, one action, then another and another—never settling, never making excuses, keeping the pressure on is the only way to get your business and your life to the level you desire. Progress over perfection.

I am working my DAMN Plan, and the damn thing is working! You can do it, too. For a bit of extra help with squirrels and other focus problems, head over to the sidebar.

Once you make
a decision, the
universe conspires
to make it happen.

—Ralph Waldo Emerson

Sidebar
Focus And Other Squirrel Problems

I nudged my granddaughter, pushing her little body into a position that helped me find straps A, C, and F to correspond with locks B, D, and E. It was a state-of-the-art car seat from hell. We were going to the grocery store a mile down the road, not commencing a moon launch, for Pete's sake! This was so much easier, although maybe not safer, thirty years ago.

Find strap A and insert in lock B. Pull strap C down firmly and secure to lock D. I nudged. She wiggled. I pulled. She twisted. I turned—all the while engaged in an especially important conversation about the laser beam of sunlight bouncing around the car. Nudging, wiggling, chattering, we were making headway until, from somewhere behind the scenes, a sergeant-like voice commanded, "Focus, Kami, focus."

I craned my neck to see under my armpit. Squinting one eye, I caught a brief glimpse of the demanding adult. My granddaughter cuddled my face in her small hands and whispered, "Oh, Grandma, focus is not my middle name!"

Gently kissing her as grandmas do, I whispered, "Not mine, either."

If focus is not your middle name, you are in good company. No one likes to admit it, but we all lose focus from time to time. Even the most ambitious among us know how incredibly difficult it is to maintain a high level of concentration, especially when we get tired, are bored doing a tedious project, or new shiny objects beckon us to come hither. *Squirrel!*

Yet, we know the fulfillment of promises and attainment of our goals is totally dependent on our ability to focus and take consistent action aligned with our priorities. When we allow distractions to constantly interrupt our workflow, we lose precious time and money, not to mention the mental toll and feelings of worthlessness that accompany our inability to stay on task.

Did you ever ignite a piece of paper with the sun's rays laser-focused through a magnifying glass when you were a kid? It took a steady hand and patience. Soon, smoldering embers ignited. Pretty cool!

Imagine what it would feel like if you could be that laser focused. I know you could illuminate the whole world and the world is waiting for you to do just that. So let's figure this out.

Focus, like time, has been a serious nemesis of mine. It doesn't take much to make me *squirrel.* Staying focused took a strong injection of the dreaded D: Discipline. First, I had to create a kick-ass motivator that would be stronger than the next shiny object.

When I whispered, *"no more,"* I made an irrevocable pledge to myself, born of a strong belief in my capacity and a clear vision of the rewards that come from focus and consistent action. If you are truly committed to what you have established as your kick-ass motivator, you are firm in your willingness and believe in the value of your business offering, you *will* focus.

The number one tip I can give you for staying focused is to quit saying you struggle with focus or that you can't! *Yes*, you can. Our minds believe what we feed them. If you keep saying, "Staying focused is tough," you will believe it and create a self-fulfilling prophecy. Quit saying you can't focus.

Then set your mind on the positive consequences of pushing back against the millions of things that want to steal your attention. If you have not written this vision into your motivator, go back and add it. If a two-week cruise is your motivator, let that vision beat back those squirrels. If living life without regrets is your motivator, come to see all those squirrels as little ghosts of your regrets! Silly, I know, but this is a mind game. You will become what you think. You will do exactly what you tell yourself you are able to do. You will be *built by actions taken—not by the time spent on the sidelines* making excuses about your squirrel problems.

So let me ask you, "Do you *really* want to find freedom, love, and money in your business?"

If the answer is yes, the choice of how you spend your time and what distractions you allow is all yours. I am not making light of focus problems. They are real. I know the challenges, but I can truly say that when I got over my squirrel-chasing habit and made the determined-decision to focus, my stress level went down and my productivity went up.

Here's what worked for me:

- Focus on one desired outcome at a time. Multitasking can be a superpower, but more often it will be your kryptonite.

- Make a *doable* "I will" list and stick to it. When a shiny object presents itself, ask yourself, "Will this create the desired outcome I am working to achieve, or is it a distraction?"

- Budget time—don't squeeze high-priority work into leftover time. Give your most important work your best time, when your attention is at its peak, and you can stay in the flow without interruptions.

- Talk to your family and friends. Tell them your plan. Share why this is so important to you. Enlist their help to keep you focused and not be one of your distractions. Then when you say, "No, I am working," they can be supportive. If not, you need to tackle their lack of support head on; don't use it as an excuse to put your dreams aside.

- Work in an environment conducive to your optimal focus, turning off electronic notifications and shutting down whatever distracts you.

- Work in spurts! Set a timer and don't move until you are done with your nonnegotiable tasks.

Reward yourself with a healthy treat or a walk outside in the sun *only* when you are done.

- Leave time open. You must have time to *just be.* Time to refill your emotional gas tank is proven to increase productivity and focus.

- Get outside—exercise, walk, or just enjoy some sunshine.

- Eat right.

- Get six to eight hours of sleep.

One of the simplest focus tools I used in the beginning was keeping my motivator front and center. Combining the concepts of a soul collage and vision board, I kept my motivator as the wallpaper on my cell phone. This simple tool was a visual reminder that kept me focused and determined. It's probably time that I make a new one, since I have grown, and my goals and motivators have changed.

—— REFLECTION ——

Is Focus Your Middle Name?

#1 Truth. What do I believe about my capacity?

_____

_____

_____

#2 Truth. Do I have a clear vision of the rewards I will receive from acting on my determined-decisions?

_____

_____

_____

#3 Truth. Is my motivator strong enough to keep me focused?

_____

_____

_____

#4 Truth. Have I given my motivator permission to kick my backside if I backslide?

_____

_____

_____

I have said it many times already, but here it goes again: *Ask for help.* From my perspective, investing in a coach to keep me focused and on track has given me a higher return on my investment than all my student loans combined.

Do. Or do not.
There is no try.

—Yoda

M Is For Mind Your Business

Yes, mind your own business! You are the boss. You are authorized and responsible for making business decisions—if you want your business baby to grow up, you need to, like any parent, do your best to make determined-decisions for its welfare at all times. The only way you can do that is if you know your numbers.

If I jumped out of the bushes today, mic in hand and said, "I have this check right here for one million dollars. It's all yours *if* you tell me your financial position."

Note: Please don't ever give out your financial information to someone who jumps out of the bushes requesting it, even for one million dollars. But humor me and take a moment to ponder these questions.

Could you tell me which of your offerings is most profitable?

Could you tell me your cost of operations—your fixed and variable expenses? Are they in line with your sales?

Could you tell me whether or not you are actually making money?

Would you know how to answer these questions? Or would you just say, "I think I am doing ok. Or I might be in trouble; I don't know."

If working on your financials is your least-favorite thing to do in your business, you are not alone. Remember, 84 percent of businesses operate without a financial plan.

You might meticulously track every penny to keep the department of revenue and the IRS at bay, but that's pretty much it. If so, you are not alone. You might procrastinate sitting down with your numbers because you are afraid of what the truth might be. You are not alone. You are so gosh-darn busy that you just don't have time to do your books. You are not alone, though that's a lousy, stress-inducing excuse. You might be really pretty good at the financial piece but would like to be more confident in making financial decisions that increase freedom, love, and money. You are not alone.

Regardless of your status, no beating yourself with a wet noodle. Just simply ask for help. No guilt. No shame. No nothing. Not knowing reduces confidence and increases stress. That is true of everything in life, especially money and our financial position. If you know that you have sufficient cash on hand to weather a storm, you breathe. You create. You thrive. You fulfill your mission. If you don't know, you worry, and that takes up all your good brain cells, creativity drops like a rock, and so do you.

I need to pull the No Excuses Card right here and now! There is a simple, nonnegotiable rule for minding your business. It will change the way you treat your business and will save you an inordinate amount of time on April 15 and every other day of the year: *No commingling!*

No, this is not free dating advice. This is business advice. Do not commingle your personal money with business money. Open a separate, legit business bank account *just* for your business. It does not matter how small you think you are or the number of transactions you initiate. If you want to have a "real" business, you need to conduct it like one.

Was that strong enough? I'm not kidding, doggone it. You have a business, not a hobby. You must clearly be able to see your business money *daily* and it is damn hard to see it when it is mixed in with transactions from McDonald's and Costco.

Without exception, this is nonnegotiable:

1. All (and I mean *all*) cash, checks, credit card receipts and direct deposits coming into your business must (and I mean *must*) go into a separate business bank account.

2. All (and I mean *all*) expenses must be paid out of that same separate business bank account or dedicated business credit card (which then gets paid for out of your business checking account).

What? Does it seem like I'm shouting? I am, and I won't apologize. Of all the craziness in the world of small business, running your personal and business expenses and income together is the craziest! Don't do it.

Okay, breathe.

Are you ready for the next nonnegotiable rule of minding your business?

Monitor your cash flow or die!

On top of having all your income and expenses going in and out of your business bank account, monitoring your cash flow is a nonnegotiable action that you must do consistently—sometimes daily.

In my thirty-some years of business coaching, when the unexpected or uncontrollable has happened—recessions, viruses (human and otherwise) death, birth, road construction—I have seen time and again that businesses that track cash flow are able to navigate unknown waters with confidence. It is the difference between surviving and curling up in a chair and shutting down. And those same businesses that are minding their cash flow, when times aren't so tough, quickly bounce back into the thriving category.

In accounting terms, cash flow is the difference between the cash you have at the beginning of the month (beginning cash) and the cash available at the end of the month (ending cash). If you have money left at the end of the month, you have positive cash flow. If you have too much month left at the end of the money (maybe like your personal budget), you have negative cash flow. You cannot operate with negative cash for long unless you have an unlimited reserve (or a one million dollar check pops out of the bushes).

Cash flow is the money coming into your business through your sales/services or capital injections (loans and owner contributions) and the money going out of your business to pay the bills, debts and you; most importantly is the timing of that money.

CHAPTER 5

According to multiple studies, 82 percent of businesses that fail to succeed reported negative or no cash flow as the reason. No business owner wants to become the poster child for that statistic. Yet many business owners fail to prioritize managing their money—minding their business—despite the fact that doing so is a huge stress reliever and the first line of defense against the unknown.

I've personally been in cash flow hell! It looks a bit different for every business. For many growing and emerging small businesses, it might look something like this:

- Payroll is ten days away, and your bank account is bouncing in the zero zone. You're scared and ashamed that you will have to tell your staff they won't get paid on Friday unless you can get your slow-paying clients to pay you. To make it worse, the last thing you want your clients to think is that you are desperate, so you keep putting off those collection calls.

- You haven't paid yourself in a month of Sundays. There is always another bill with higher priority. Even if you could pay yourself, it would be less than minimum wage. Your fun meter is bouncing in the zero zone, and your old day job with a Friday paycheck is starting to look good.

- You have been so busy delivering your product or service that you put marketing activities on the back burner. Now your pipeline is empty, and cultivating new business usually takes two months, which means there will be a huge gap in the cash coming in and, most likely, cash going out will balloon.

- You are presented with the opportunity of a lifetime, but you have no cash or credit to fund the expansion you'd need in order to capitalize on it. You can't do a darn thing; you have been paying late because the timing of money coming in and going out is whacked. Your business credit score has tanked. You are afraid to face the banker for a loan. You feel like a failure.

I have learned (albeit the hard way a time or two) the importance of cash flow and keeping up with your financials. I, too, have been so busy working *in* my business that I've failed to work *on* it. I've spent all my time serving my clients, creating new products, and making sales and neglected to see whether I was actually making money. I've been ashamed. I've gotten so far behind on my accounting that I didn't have the courage to ask for help. Ouch!

No Excuses Card time! *Do as I say, not as I did.* Let me save you some of that pain. Track your numbers consistently (daily).

The primary goal of cash flow management and your job as the boss of your business is to control the cash that goes out while increasing the cash coming in. That's a two-sided deal. All too often, the focus is placed strictly on one or the other as a means to improve cash flow: more money in *or* less money out. Yet, minding both sides is the sweet spot where freedom, love, and money coexist.

If you can earn more while working fewer hours and spending less, you will find the trifecta. The one-two-three punch that can get you there in the shortest period of time is when you:

1. Prioritize resources to build relationships with your *ideal clients*. These are high-value clients who recognize your value and are willing to pay for it.

2. Get rid of your fears and establish a price/fee structure that reflects the value you bring. Don't settle. Imagine the impossible. Ask for the unlikely. You might just get it. Damn!

3. Mind your money coming in and going out. Help people pay you on time to maintain good relationships. Pay your bills on time to maintain good credit. No buying shiny objects and gobbledygook you don't need.

Let's start with numbers one and two. Who is your ideal client? Does your fee/price structure reflect the value of your offer in your ideal clients' eyes?

Business owners attending my training events often start out saying, "*Everyone* can use these products or services." To increase sales (and sometimes out of fear), sheer survival instinct kicks in and you might take any client or customer with a pulse. If you live in small markets, a tight-knit neighborhood, or a rural community, you may feel some pressure to serve everyone, even when you know that some (maybe even quite a few) are not making you money or, worse yet, are costing you money.

Maybe you have a big heart, or maybe you are afraid of what people will think if you charge your *real* value price. I get it. I shared with you that I increased the investment (fee) that my clients made in my services 300 percent over two years. My momma heart got in the way more than once before I made that leap; I was afraid of hurting people. I was afraid of losing friendships. But in the end, I remembered a simple rule one of my mentors told me a long time ago:

People have friends. Businesses have customers.

If you can't pay your bills, you go out of business. Then you ain't helping nobody! It's the old, "put *your* mask on first" airplane analogy. If you, as the business, aren't strong, you, the friend, can't afford to help. As hard as it might be, especially in the beginning when your biggest supporters will be family and friends, it is important to keep your business and personal life separate when it comes to finances.

To start examining your current client base and setting yourself up to attract higher-value clients, ask yourself:

- Who am I currently serving? Are they ideal or just ok?

- Who *is* my ideal client? What is their pain and pleasure? Does my offering alleviate their pain or increase their pleasure? If yes, what is stopping me from building a relationship with this target market?

- Does my fee/price structure—the investment that I am asking clients to make—reflect my value? Remember, it's all about perception. Value is in the eye of the beholder. Remember them peaches.

- What do I need to do to build relationships with this high-value market? Have I budgeted my time, and do I have the discipline to conduct my relationship-building activities consistently every day?

One of the best determined-decisions you will ever make is to tighten up and focus on attracting and serving your *ideal client.* If you choose a small niche of high-value clients, you can tailor your offering and message to them. You will be able to give your ideal clients your best because you will not be too busy serving *everyone.*

In the end, getting to work with your ideal clients is all about belief in your value. I said earlier that one of the most important things you can do is align yourself with someone who believes in you more than you believe in yourself. Find yourself a coach who will be that person and hold your feet to the fire until you believe. Then, and only then, will your ideal client believe in you and invest.

Knowing the value of your offer and knowing your ideal client's unique pain points could move you from a negative cash position to a positive cash position. In other words, setting your value price could get you out of the hole. Let's play with a cash flow scenario about how pricing affects cash flow.

Meet Mary. She is a newly minted business owner, having started her coaching practice after years in the corporate sphere. Like someone you might know, she just simply grabbed her hourly rate of $50 out of the air, basing that decision on the salary she earned as an employee. Hmmm? This may not go so well. She was realistic about her billable hours, factoring in marketing time. Eighty-nine hours out of 170 hours in the average month seemed doable. She calculated her fixed-cost budget at $4,311, factoring in what it would cost for space, marketing, and a very part-time assistant. After talking with a few other solopreneurs in her networking group, she estimated that her variable costs would be about 30 percent of sales, so she added 4 percent to be on the safe side. I am barely making this up. This is so real.

Let's see what happens when we put all these numbers into a basic cash flow worksheet.

	Month 1	Month 2	Month 3	Month 4	Month 5	Month 6
Beginning Cash Balance	0	–1,373	–2,747	–4,121	–5,994	–7,418
Cash Receipts						
Cash Received from Sales	4,450	4,450	4,450	4,450	4,450	4,450
Total Cash Available	4,450	3,076	1,703	329	–1,544	–2,968
Variable Costs						
Materials	1,513	1,513	1,513	1,513	1,513	1,513
Total Variable Costs	1,513	1,513	1,513	1,513	1,513	1,513
Operating Costs						
Marketing	500	500	500	500	500	500
Payroll, Including Taxes	2,500	2,500	2,500	2,500	2,500	2,500
Debt Principal/Interest	761	761	761	761	761	761
Legal/Professional	350	350	350	350	350	350
Office Expense	50	50	50	50	50	50
Repair/Maintenance	0	0	0	500	50	150
Insurance	150	150	150	150	150	150
Total Operating Costs	4,311	4,311	4,311	4,811	4,361	4,461
Value Pay	0	0	0	0	0	0
Total Cash Paid Out	5,824	5,824	5,824	6,324	5,874	5.974
Ending Cash Balance	**–1,374**	**–2,747**	**–4,121**	**–5,994**	**–7,418**	**–8,914**

As you can see, there is a negative cash balance right out of the gate, and the hole is getting deeper. On top of that Mary is paying herself absolutely zero. Zero Value Pay for Mary. This is Mary's truth. It happens, but it is not written in stone. Mary has choices—determined-decisions to make. She will need to change her mindset and focus on her ideal clients who value her offer.

Let's ask one of those *what ifs* we talked about in breakeven. *What if* she increased the investment she is asking her clients to make by just $30 per hour?

	Month 1	Month 2	Month 3	Month 4	Month 5	Month 6
Beginning Cash Balance	0	−1,296	−1,593	−1,889	−1,686	−1,932
Cash Receipts						
Cash Received from Sales	7,120	7,120	7,120	7,120	7,120	7,120
Total Cash Available	7,120	8,416	8,713	9,009	8,806	9,052
Variable Costs						
Materials	1,513	1,513	1,513	1,513	1,513	1,513
Total Variable Costs	1,513	1,513	1,513	1,513	1,513	1,513
Operating Costs						
Marketing	500	500	500	500	500	500
Payroll, Including Taxes	2,500	2,500	2,500	2,500	2,500	2,500
Debt Principal/Interest	761	761	761	761	761	761
Legal/Professional	350	350	350	350	350	350
Office Expense	50	50	50	50	50	50
Repair/Maintenance	0	0	0	500	50	150
Insurance	150	150	150	150	150	150
Total Operating Costs	4,311	4,311	4,311	4,811	4,361	4,461
Value Pay	0	1,000	1,000	1,000	1,000	1,000
Total Cash Paid Out	5,824	6,824	6,824	7,324	6,874	6,974
Ending Cash Balance	1,296	1,593	1,889	1,686	1,932	2,079

It's just about magical! All other costs remain the same. Mary gets to *at least* pay herself $1,000/month. It's a start. There are many more determined-decisions she can make to get paid her value. It will be up to her. She is authorized and responsible. She's the boss.

Whether you are a solopreneur or have staff, you are responsible for the financial decisions of your business. No excuses. With a wide array of accounting, point-of-sale and tracking systems as close as your phone, I cannot think of one good excuse for not knowing your numbers. You can't make future determined-decisions about the direction of your business if you don't know the results of your current actions.

You could keep doing the same thing over and over expecting different results, but that's just plain crazy.

Here are some discovery questions you might ask right off the bat to test your money management systems:

- Like your personal committed decisions, do you have a system that tracks your payables? Do you manage your vendor relationships, or just hope they will deliver? Do you negotiate or accept whatever they offer?

- Are your expenses and purchasing habits in alignment with your determined-decisions? Will the professional subscriptions, memberships, applications, or extra paraphernalia enhance your ability to achieve your goals? Would it be better to hire contractors or to have staff? Do you need a permanent office space or can you cowork? Are your purchasing decisions based on wants or needs?

- How do you use credit? Are you using the right money— bank loan, credit card, supplier credit—to your best advantage? Are you building or taking care of your personal or business credit, so you have options? Do you have a relationship with your banker?

- How are you managing your accounts receivable? Do you *hope* people will pay on time, or are you asking for what you need when you need it? Do you have a contract or service agreement that clearly spells out the expectations of both parties? Does the contract or agreement state the value you will provide and the Value Price or investment your customer will make?

Let's play with another cash flow scenario to see how managing or not managing your accounts receivable, hiring and purchasing decisions can affect your cash position.

Meet Nikki. She is extraordinary, downright brilliant as a marketing manager in her industry. Feeling undervalued at her place of employment, she exits stage left, with many of her existing clients following her. With her expertise and reputation, there is no shortage of clients. She gets overwhelmed and hires *some* help! She bases her decision only on the fact that she is overwhelmed and needs help. She does not review the impact of her hiring decision on sales or cash flow.

Oh! Did I tell you that she is a single woman and relies solely on the income from the business to pay her personal expenses? She must make at least $3,500 per month.

By month four, even though sales have been steady, she is no longer able to pay herself and she *needed* to purchase some computer equipment for $2,500. Then because she was so gosh-darn busy, she added yet another part-time person. By the end of month six, she has gone ninety days without pay. It was definitely time for Nikki to get a handle on her cash flow and work *on* her business, not just *in* it. The truth was staring her in the face. To say she was frazzled was an understatement, but the decisions had been hers. Knowing the truth will allow her to make better determined-decisions by the numbers from here forward.

	Month 1	Month 2	Month 3	Month 4	Month 5	Month 6
Beginning Cash Balance	0	600	450	967	−183	1,950
Cash Receipts						
Cash Received from Sales	0	5,000	10,000	10,000	12,500	15,000
Cash Injections from Loans/Owner	5,000					
Total Cash Receipts	5,000	5,000	10,000	10,000	12,500	15,000
Total Cash Available	5,000	5,600	10,450	10,967	12,317	16,950
Fixed Costs						
Marketing	1,500	500	500	500	500	500
Payroll, Including Taxes	0	0	4,333	6,500	8,667	8,667
Debt Principal/Interest	0	450	450	450	450	450
Legal/Professional	350	500	500	500	500	500
Office Expense	50	50	50	50	50	50
Repair/Maintenance	0	0	0	500	50	150
Real Estate Tax	0	0	0	0	0	2,500
Insurance	500	150	150	150	150	150
Capital Purchases	0	0	0	2,500	0	0
Reserve and/or Escrow	0	0	0	0	0	0
Owner's Value Pay	2,000	3,500	3,500	0	0	0
Total Fixed Costs	4,400	5,150	9,483	11,150	10,367	12,967
Ending Cash Balance	600	450	967	−183	1,950	3,983

Let's see what some relatively simple tweaks can do. First, *what if* she made it policy to have her clients make a 20 percent deposit before commencing work on their projects? This would speed up receivables and frankly is an industry norm for many independent contractors and service-based businesses.

Second, let's take a look at that payroll. Nikki had made somewhat of a knee-jerk decision to hire when she added her two full-time people. Hiring is a challenge at best, but when you are not analyzing the impact of your hiring decisions, it can be a disaster. She should have asked one question. Are the people being hired increasing sales/productivity or using up precious time, energy and money without contributing to the bottom line? Very simply, whether its hiring contractors or staff, all persons working for your company must be contributing members. If they do not increase revenues in some way, why are you hiring them?

Nikki wanted her dream of freedom, love, and money so she made hard decisions about staffing and with confidence in her decision, she had no problem requesting down payments. After all, she is downright brilliant at what she does and damn well worth it!

	Month 1	Month 2	Month 3	Month 4	Month 5	Month 6
Beginning Cash Balance	0	3,100	5,450	5,967	2,567	4,617
Cash Receipts						
Cash Received from Sales	0	2,500	5,000	5,000	6,250	7,500
Cash from Deposits	2,500	5,000	5,000	6,250	7,500	7,500
Total Cash Receipts	7,500	7,500	10,000	11,250	13,750	15,000
Total Cash Available	7,500	10,600	15,450	17,217	16,317	19,617
Fixed Costs						
Marketing	1,500	500	500	500	500	500
Payroll, Including Taxes	0	0	4,333	6,500	6,500	6,500
Debt Principal/Interest	0	450	450	450	450	450
Legal/Professional	350	500	500	500	500	500
Office Expense	50	50	50	50	50	50
Repair/Maintenance	0	0	0	500	50	150
Real Estate Tax	0	0	0	0	0	2,500
Insurance	500	150	150	150	150	150
Capital Purchases	0	0	0	2,500	0	0
Reserve and/or Escrow	0	0	0	0	0	0
Owner's Value Pay	2,000	3,500	3,500	3,500	3,500	3,500
Total Fixed Costs	4,400	5,150	9,483	14,650	11,700	14,300
Ending Cash Balance	3,100	5,450	5,967	2,567	4,617	5,317

Both Mary's and Nikki's scenarios are fairly simple. Many cash flow decisions are much more complex, and many are just this simple. The numbers may or may not look like your own. Regardless, pricing correctly, managing costs, and controlling the timing of cash coming in can make a major difference in your business and how you feel about it. Getting paid your value is really nice!

I've asked a lot of questions in this last section. By now, you may be wanting to shake me and shout, "Just tell me what to do!" I hear you. Sorry. Not sorry. Every DAMN Plan evolves as a series of answers to a series of questions. Your business is unique. Your starting point is where *you* are, here and now. To identify that starting point, you must learn to ask yourself questions. No settling for what is. No shoulder shrugs or complacency. Get out your damn attitude and take it for a walk. Question everything. Frankly, you can sum it all up and get better at minding your business by asking those essential questions:

How are we doing?
What can we do better?

These two questions are at the heart of what it takes to be successful. They are the essence of what it means to work *on* your business and not just *in* it.

Now that I have yelled at you about your banking/accounting habits and threatened you to manage your cash flow or die, go to kimnagle.com/cashflow and check out my Cash Flow with Confidence Course where I will teach you all about how you can get your cash flowing. As part of the course you will also receive my DAMN Cash Flow Projection Tool.

Using this tool on a regular basis can help you:

1. Plan your spending

2. Identify the upfront cash needed to increase sales

3. Plan for unexpected cash emergencies

4. Figure out what you must do to get paid your value

Beyond that, knowing your financial position and minding your cash flow will build confidence. Even if things don't look so good from time to time, you will know the actions that must be taken and be resolved to take them.

Wherever you are, and whatever brought you here, you are not alone, and you *do not* have to go it alone. You don't need to know everything to be successful. You just need to be courageous enough to ask for help.

Let's talk about one more thing you need to do to mind your business: Surround yourself with a great team.

I have made jokes, bad ones now that I think of it, about knowing just enough to be dangerous. Truth be told, there have been times when I didn't even know what I didn't know. Worse, I was embarrassed to admit I was lost and needed help. What would people say? They obviously would think less of me if they knew the truth.

Half the time, doing my own accounting was more about hiding than it was about the cost of hiring an accountant. It was only when I was willing to be honest with myself, admitted I couldn't go it alone and got the courage to ask for assistance that help arrived.

I am making a big deal about not going it alone, asking for help, and being honest simply because it has been a barrier to success for me and so many others.

I have seen too many businesses collapse because the owner waited too long to ask for help. For those willing to share and be honest, asking for help was the difference between settling for less and coming to resent their businesses, or getting paid their value and falling in love with it.

If you have completed the five steps to making determined-decisions, you have done the hard work of getting your numbers out of your head and onto paper. You have made your first determined-decisions. These decisions are all yours, and you will ultimately be responsible for their outcomes. However, rather than carrying the weight of the world with only your strong legs, your best bet will be to put together a team of people who can look objectively at your numbers and your decisions. This will be your next courageous move.

I understand that it requires trust. I understand that there may be some pain if you allow your team to be brutally honest with you. I understand. Oh, boy, do I understand!

I remember the day that my business partner, who also happens to be my daughter, went toe-to-toe with me and said, "No, I don't agree!"

Oh, my!

I was holding down both of my hands behind my back. On one hand, I knew she was right and I was wrong. On the other hand, it was my idea. I loved my idea even if it *was* wrong. I think you might know the feelings that go with that scene. Let me tell you, all the feelings were there.

In one fell swoop, I was proud as heck that I had raised a strong daughter with a damn attitude; I finally got out of my own way, truly becoming a boss when I was willing to ask for and receive advice.

Building a team is not necessarily about hiring employees or taking on partners. Our business teams represent the skills, talents, and services that we need to successfully operate. Here is my short list of possible team members:

- Banker
- Accountant
- Tax specialist
- Financial planner
- Insurance agent
- Marketing professional
- Web designer
- Copyeditor
- Social media manager
- Virtual assistant
- Business coach

If you are hiring a paid contractor, choosing a banker, insurance agent, or business coach, make sure your decision is logical, not emotional. All too often, small business owners and independents hire the first contractor or choose the first service provider who comes their way. They neglect the due diligence required to vet and get the best for their money.

Here are just a few rules that I have for hiring and building your team.

Rule #1: Don't hire (or get free help from) friends and family unless they really are the best person for the job.

If you do hire close associates and family members, there must still be a contractual agreement and clear written understanding of the expectations of all parties. Plan an out. For my daughter and me, we have already agreed that if this business relationship ever interferes with our mother-daughter relationship, we will tap out. This is the only way that these relationships will remain intact when the going gets tough.

Rule #2: Don't offhandedly say that you can't afford to contract or hire.

This is a numbers issue about time and money. Don't make assumptions without crunching the numbers. What is the value of your time? What would the value be if projects got done faster? What would be the value of having another set of eyes, ears, and brain cells on a project? After you consider all of these angles, you might realize that the DIY method will actually be more costly than hiring out.

Rule #3: Only hire if it will improve the financial position of the business.

The only expensive help is help that does not improve your business and its financial position. All too often, small businesses fall into a trap of thinking that they need an employee because other businesses like theirs have employees, or the company they used to work for had those employee positions. Crunch your numbers.

When choosing your team, interview contractors and potential staff members carefully, remembering they will be working for *you* and helping you pursue *your dream*. Ask for referrals from people you know, like, and trust. Lastly, if you are not comfortable with a potential team member, thank them for their time and move on. This is a great time to remind you of my mentor's rule with a tweak.

People have friends. Businesses have teams of qualified professionals.

We have discussed making determined-decisions, acting consistently and minding your business, all of which encompass the prime tenet of The DAMN Plan: the truth—fact and reality.

Our determined-decisions are decisions based on the truth and backed up with the resolve and willingness to act. When you mind your businesses, you keep track of the truth, the facts, and reality and use this information to make determined-decisions.

There's still one more DAMN letter to discuss. N is for No Excuses, which may be your biggest truth of all. But, before we go there, I want you to head over to the sidebar. There is a quick truth we need to talk about. After reading this story, you may consider firing yourself.

Sidebar
You Might Not Be The Best Person For The Job

Remember when I said "The only expensive help is help that does not improve your business and its financial position"? Well, what would you think if I told you that maybe *you* are the one costing your business money? Sounds pretty damn blunt, doesn't it? Hear me out before you shred this book and toss the pieces into the fire.

Knowing the strengths you bring to your business and maximizing them will be key to getting yourself paid your value. Sometimes, the best management decision you can make is to hand over the reins of some part of your business to a more qualified person. One of the toughest realities you as a business owner may have to face is admitting that you may not be the best person for a job—especially when it's a job *you* created. No one's story proves the value of making that difficult decision better than John's.

As a young man, John's achievements earned him a position on stages across the world. Since childhood, it seemed as if he had strategically plotted his course, complete with an academic scholarship, worldwide competitions, inventions, and now his own business. Despite his early success, there was never a boast or brag—just pure, unadulterated excitement and commitment to excellence.

One afternoon, I watched him as we ate our lunch and listened to other people's random conversations. Something was very different today. Waiting for the appropriate lull, I asked how things were going. Silently, he motioned me outside, away from examining eyes and ears. In the shelter of a quiet spot where souls can be confidential, John began to lay out his current reality.

The honeymoon was over. He had ridden the start-up wave high, hiring friends and associates to support what appeared to be endless demand and interest. By his own admission, he had been a reckless spender when money was flush. He felt remorse about purchasing equipment and things he thought were essential for his businesses but maybe weren't necessary.

For a moment between confessions, his eyes flashed with fresh excitement as he talked about the new product he and his team were building. With a heavy sigh, he admitted to not acting on the marketing and sales plans we had formulated. His posture and the look on his face said it all. He would rather be back in the shop—working with the team, creating and developing new products— than making sales calls. Sales calls equaled *pain* in his mind.

Now he was looking down the barrel of mounting debt and financial obligations coming due. Arms folded and unable to sit down, he attempted to create a self-protective barrier between us. From four feet away, the ache in his core, his very soul, was palpable. As he spoke, it became apparent the angst he was feeling was not the fear of failing, but the fear of not proceeding.

He turned away slightly to catch a tear. Some of you reading this book know the feeling. A touch of nausea. The pang of heartache. The pains are real and symptomatic of the driving force within those of us who dare to dance in the playground of possibility.

I wanted to thin the air a bit and say something like, "The force is strong within you, my son," but it was no laughing matter. These were real, heavy, raw emotions that needed to be worked through in order to protect John from losing his dream. Stern empathy was needed. I asked, "How do you feel about your business? Do you still want it?"

His response, spoken with humility, confirmed my intuition. "I can't imagine myself doing anything else."

John was a genius—a talented creative who absolutely abhorred making sales calls, so he just didn't do them. Furthermore, he had so much passion for his product that he was constantly promising more than he could deliver for a price he couldn't afford to charge. John needed a sales manager.

His first step was letting go, which for many entrepreneurs is the hardest step of all. First, we are control freaks. That's why we are in business for ourselves.

His next step was finding the right person for the job.

Last, he needed to let his new partners do what they did best, so John could do what he did best and loved the most.

Sweet! That's really why we start our businesses, so we can do what we do best.

———— REFLECTION ————

Are You Willing To Ask For And Receive Help?

1. In which areas of your business could you use help?

_____

_____

_____

2. What are the skills needed to successfully operate your business? Who has them? How much will it cost to obtain the skills your business needs?

Skills	Who	Cost

3. What is stopping you from getting the help you need?

_____

_____

_____

4. Are you ready to receive help?

_____

_____

_____

Ninety-nine percent of the failures come from people who have the habit of making excuses.

—George Washington Carver

6

CHAPTER

N Is For No Excuses!

have already said "no excuses" at least a dozen times in this damn book! Do you get my point? Excuses are like anchors holding you down, keeping you tethered in the same spot. I have made enough excuses in my lifetime to fill a boat, maybe the Titanic! You know what happened to the Titanic.

No Excuses! I have saved this discussion for last because, when you quit making excuses and abdicating your life to something or someone else, you will break free and grow. When you forgive yourself and stop ruminating over your woulda-shoulda-couldas, you will find the freedom, love, and money you seek.

Your time is now! *Now* is a recognition that you are here as a result of your struggles and successes. You are here as a result of all your lessons learned. They have built you and prepared you to deliver on your divine gift.

I didn't always believe this. When I was putting together my own DAMN Plan, I struggled with very real grief over lost time. I beat myself up, tore myself down, and came up with more woulda-shoulda-couldas than I care to admit. I was holding myself in a state of unforgiveness and regret, which anchored my ass to the past. I was a prisoner in a cage of excuses, blaming and shaming.

It took me a while to admit to needing help, but sitting in the ER in unbelievable, stress-induced pain made it impossible to ignore. I had to decide to make determined-decisions. I had to act. I had to pay attention and mind my business. Above all, I had to take responsibility for my action or inaction and claim authority over my business and my life.

I needed to quit being a *but*-head. (No, I did not just call myself a butthead.)

In the introduction, I gave you the definition of the truth. The one thing that can negate the truth is a but. *Buts* are like excuses on steroids. You say them, write them, and think them all the time without even realizing it. And, suddenly, they're the first thing that comes to mind when an opportunity presents itself. But-head conversations go something like this:

"I want to make this business work, *but* . . ."

"I want to make more money, *but* . . ."

"I want to work less so I can [fill in your personal priorities], *but* . . ."

Listen up, I'm pulling the No Excuses Card. *Stop being a but-head! Don't say or think with a* but *in your head.*

Over the years, I have worked with a lot of but-heads—the biggest of whom was probably me. The best gift I have ever given myself was time—the time I needed to work on my own mindset and mental health. Through this process I was told time and time again, "Every time you insert 'but,' you negate everything you just said. In other words, Kim, if you say, 'I want to live my best life, *but* . . .' and then insert every conceivable excuse on the planet, the truth is you really *don't* want to live your best life. Period."

Too often, a *but* gets thrown in because there is no real commitment or willingness to do whatever it takes. A *but*, you think, will let you off the hook if you don't take action, stay focused and disciplined. It won't. It just buries your anchor deeper into the weeds, muck, and mud.

We all have real life reasons for why this might not be the best time or place to start or grow a business. That's okay. If you are making that decision based on fact and reality, that's wisdom. On the other hand, if you are going to make excuses, save yourself some time and energy and just admit that you really don't want your business.

I know it's a daily challenge to keep the *but* out of your head. All I can say is stop it. Every time a but shows up in your thoughts or conversation, kick its ass with the truth—your truth. No blame. No shame. No *buts* about it.

Here's how you can change the conversation when *buts* threaten to derail you. Simply replace "want" with "decided" then the "but" with "and."

"I decided to make this business work, *and* I am willing to do what it takes."

"I decided to make more money, *and* I will reduce costs or increase revenue."

"I decided to work less so I can [fill in your personal priorities] *and* I will write my DAMN Plan to find high-value clients that pay my fee *and* keep costs under control."

Once you speak your truth without being a but-head, you will claim authority and responsibility for your own best life.

From here on out, there are no excuses. Go get your numbers. Do the research. Ask the questions. Make your determined-decisions and act consistently. Boom!

Your time is now. Prioritize your time to make it happen. Successful business owners work *on* their businesses more than they work *in* their businesses. It's a fact, and it is not up for debate. For heaven's sake, quit being a but-head and get it done.

We may not know each other personally (yet) nevertheless I know the feelings you might have. I know the angst of wanting something so bad and it seems like it is always just out of your reach. All I can say is DAMN! Take that next step. If not now, when?

Let's talk about it in our last sidebar.

Sidebar
If Not Now, When?

Not thirty years ago, when judging by world standards, I should have had my act together. Instead, I was making a *comeback* after the death of my second daughter and losing everything I had to medically induced bankruptcy. *I learned resilience.*

Not twenty-five years ago, when I started three different businesses, did OK, but fell short of my wildest dreams, I *learned* more than a few lessons that have informed my best business decisions the hard way. *I learned to do better.*

Not twenty years ago, when the truth about my screwed up personal life was staring me in the face and I perhaps should have made a life-changing decision but couldn't because it just didn't seem that black and white, *I learned that not deciding is the worst decision you can make.*

Not fifteen years ago, when things were fine, living was reasonably easy as an empty nester and I could've fully launched my dream, *I learned not to settle down in my comfort zone—there's no magic there!*

Not ten years ago, when my mom's passing left me with more time but a nagging question, "Why haven't you done what you said you would always do?" *I learned to value myself and my time.*

Frankly, struggle and success are companions on the entrepreneurial journey and life in general. This fact is found in a simple lesson my dad taught me on one of our many walks in the woods by the headwaters of the Mississippi River.

We had found a monarch caterpillar, and of course I wanted to take it home, put it in a jar and "make" myself a butterfly. Dad gathered leaves from the milkweed plants and helped me carefully put this poor, unsuspecting critter in a jar with breathing holes poked into the lid. We set up a camera and took time-lapse photos around the clock. *This would be a champion science fair presentation*, I thought.

Every day, I carefully checked on my caterpillar and watched as it proceeded through its metamorphosis. One day, a small opening appeared in the chrysalis. I watched my butterfly for several hours as it struggled to force its body through the little hole.

And then it stopped, half in and half out. "Dad! My butterfly is dying. It needs help!"

I wanted so badly to free the butterfly, to release it from its pain, but Dad stopped me and told me a story.

There once was a girl, he said, who thought she should help her butterfly. She took a pair of scissors and snipped away the remaining chrysalis. Her butterfly emerged easily, but its body was swollen and its wings were shriveled. Proud of herself, the girl watched and waited for the wings to enlarge to support the butterfly, but that never happened. The butterfly remained swollen, with tiny wings, unable to fly.

The girl (and I) did not understand that the restrictive chrysalis was part of the butterfly's divine plan. As my butterfly struggled through the small opening, it was forcing fluid from its swollen abdomen into its wings. It was growing its own wings. It had to struggle before it could take flight and fully live out its purpose.

I challenge you to see everything you have come through as pumping life into your wings so you can take flight and act *now*.

When will you quit making excuses? If not now, when? When will you recognize your divine gifts and use them to get paid your value so you can live courageously with no regrets?

──── REFLECTION ────

Excuses, Forgiveness And Other Show-Stoppers

#1 Truth. What are my top three excuses for not getting things done?

_____

_____

_____

#2 Truth. What have I learned on my life journey that has prepared me to act now?

_____

_____

_____

#3 Truth. What am I most proud of overcoming?

_____

_____

_____

#4 Truth. What do I need to forgive myself for?

_____

_____

_____

#5 Truth. What is stopping me from taking action now?

_____

_____

_____

moved into my sixties a while ago. I am not old by any stretch of the imagination; my numbers, the health kind of numbers, are great, and like my dad would say, "Everything between my ears still works real good."

I recently got the best compliment of all time—it even beats when you are with your daughter and someone asks if you are sisters. That hasn't happened yet. Damn!

But a young woman did say, "Kim, you look like you are in your prime!"

"Well, thank you very much."

Yes, I had lost a few pounds since last she saw me and got a funky new haircut, but more than that I *am* living my best life. I *am* living my mantra—my kickass motivator.

I guess it shows.

I will be courageous and master my God-given talents of speaking, writing and ideation to build a business that generates the money I need to live life on my terms. Doing so, I will model for my children and grandchildren, now and those to come, a life fully lived until the day I die. I will have no regrets. RAWR!

This is what I want for you. Regardless of where you have been, where you are right now, it's never too late, it's never too soon. Make your DAMN Plan, work your DAMN Plan. Get your damn attitude on and ride!

Acknowledgments

Mandy, thank you for being the best motivator a mom could ask for. I will not let my life lessons—*our* life lessons—be for nothing. I promise to live courageously, without regrets.

To my Michelle in heaven, thank you for leading the way to say it does not matter how many years, months or days you are given—we are all here for a reason. I will live my purpose.

Sean, thank you for teaching me to not settle, to imagine the impossible, and to ask for the unlikely. You've taken me for a crazy ride, but I am forever inspired by your tenacity.

Sandy, thank you for being my ass kicker. You held my feet to the fire and didn't let me make excuses. You did it all with the love of a daughter and a tiger taking down prey ten times its size. This book is finished because of you.

All successful people get to where they are because of their lessons learned and the mentors who inspired them. I have been blessed beyond measure by two of the best, Mark LeBlanc and Renee Rongen. I'd probably still be digging for change in the couch cushions if you hadn't helped me see my value and believed in my ability to always take one more step and dial it up a notch.

About The Author

Kim Nagle is a keynote speaker, business coach, and skilled educator and trainer who believes that knowing the truth, being curious, and maintaining a strong sense of humor are vital to building resilience and determination. She speaks and trains from the heart, having learned from every failure and success, becoming resilient and determined to do what it takes—never to settle.

As a result of creating and working her own DAMN Plan, Kim went from fighting cash flow nightmares, working for less than her value, missing out on life, and eventually landing in the ER to living her best life. By making determined-decisions, acting consistently, and minding her business—no excuses, as prescribed by *The DAMN Plan*—she has found freedom, love, and money in her business.

Her *damn* attitude, the essence of *The DAMN Plan* is a result of Kim's thirty years as a business coach and her experiences as a serial entrepreneur. She started her first business at age fourteen just so she could buy a real pair of Lee button-fly jeans and has started and grown six businesses since that first highly motivated start-up.

Her favorite business by far is Upgrow Business International, Inc. which she co-owns with her youngest daughter and kindred entrepreneurial spirit. Together, they produce and deliver training and coaching programs, online and in person, for emerging entrepreneurs and small business owners who want to start and grow profitable businesses they love.

Kim's academic studies range from theater to business and economics—she even has four college credits in sword fighting and juggling. To say the least, she is an original with a flair for the dramatic. Personality tests reveal that she is a cross between Betty White and James Bond. A forward-thinking creative businesswoman and consultant, Kim has the uncanny ability to spot opportunity and act on good ideas. Using this mindset and skill set, Kim has trained thousands and helped start and grow hundreds of small businesses.

Kim served as the director of the U.S. Small Business Administration Minnesota Women's Business Center. Her passion for entrepreneurship has led her to support the development of community development financial institutions (CDFI), business incubators, and business development programs in urban and rural communities in the Midwest.

In her role as business center director and small business developer, Kim authored comprehensive training programs to support the entrepreneurs she loves so much. Curricula include the *E-Series for Business Development, How to Budget When You Don't Have Any Money,* and *Getting Down to Business,* a guide to writing a business plan. Her latest training programs take it all to the next level and beyond. Go to kimnagle.com to learn more about training offers and coaching services.

On a personal note, Kim has raised three very entrepreneurial kids, who in turn, are raising the next generation of creative thinkers who won't settle. She revels in the time she devotes to each of her grandchildren. Whether it's playing hard at the lake, writing, drawing, sewing or concocting new recipes in the kitchen, Kim is all-in and in the moment. There will be no regrets.

Learn more about Kim

Website: kimnagle.com
Facebook: facebook.com/thedamnplan
LinkedIn: linkedin.com/in/thedamnplan
YouTube: youtube.com/thedamnplan

www.ingramcontent.com/pod-product-compliance
Lightning Source LLC
Chambersburg PA
CBHW031929190326
41519CB00007B/462